C000127356

As I Walked About

As I Walked About

A Collection
of Walking Columns
from the Ottawa Citizen

PHIL JENKINS

OTTAWA
PRESS AND
PUBLISHING

Ottawa Press and Publishing

Copyright © Philip Robert Jenkins 2020

ISBN (softcover) 978-1-988437-39-2

Cover, design, composition:
Magdalene Carson / New Leaf Publication Design

Published in Canada

No part of this book may be reproduced, stored in a retrieval system, or transmitted in any form or by any means without the prior written permission of the publisher or, in case of photocopying or other reprographic copying, a licence from Access Copyright (The Canadian Copyright Licensing Agency), 320 – 56 Wellesley Street West, Toronto, Ontario, M5S 2S3
www.accesscopyright.ca.

For Kim, step by step.

Contents

Introduction

A city is a book we learn to read by walking it.
— *Rebecca Solnit*

I can't claim to have read the book of Ottawa from cover to cover but, if its city streets are the chapters, I've turned many a page. I came by the opportunity to investigate Ottawa's streets and street life, past and present, during the later years of my quarter century as a freelance columnist at the Ottawa Citizen. Starting with Rideau Street in 2004, I followed the lead of other metropolitan cityscape writers such as E.B.White (New York), Will Self (London), Walter Benjamin (Berlin, Paris), Rebecca Solnit (San Francisco), and paced the lines of Ottawa's avenues, boulevards, lanes, paths, roads and streets, notebook in hand.

As I did so, I was concerned with both the history and the present state of the highways and byways; I was walking the streets in two tenses simultaneously, and hoped through my articles to provide readers with the same pleasurable possibility. It's a bifocal sort of way of looking at a city. On that first professional promenade down one of the city's founding streets, I realized how much I had missed when I was a casual traveller moving about Ottawa. I had walked down Rideau hundreds of times as boy and man, and had witnessed its distressing architectural lobotomy, but many of its remaining charming details had eluded me. (I was a boy in Ottawa from 1951 to 1961, and a man here from 1978 until now; half a century of putting one foot in front of the other, and counting).

I judge the vices and virtues of city streets, architectural and otherwise, with the yardstick of something called "walkability." The eye and the mind are both uninterested in the banal, the plain, the unimaginative. It is the eccentricities, the human touches, the ornamentation, the evidence of caring how a street *feels* as you move along it that determine its walkability. Whether you are a first-timer on that street, or, like me, a habitué, there must be diversity of architectural styles, of signage, of public art, of resting and gathering places, of flora and fauna, of retail outlets and restaurants and residences. And the pedestrian must come first.

Cities are cannibalistic, they eat large chunks of their own past, chewing up landscapes and buildings and regurgitating them. This municipal mastication implies a kind of hunger, the hunger to replace then with now, to recycle stale visions of a city with fresh ones. In my time in Ottawa, there has been a lot of chewing, and a whole lot more regurgitation, most of it not to my taste.

Over the period when I was walking and writing the articles you are about to read, roughly the first two decades of the 21st century, the map of the city was constantly being redrawn. Rather than edit the articles to contemporize and reflect those changes, they appear here as they did in the newspaper. Quite where they differ in detail from the present I will leave you to discover.

People take their cities, its buildings, its parks, its roads, personally. The weekly responses I received to my columns proved that. Our city is also our home; it's where we say we are from. Here is what I saw—and felt—as my hometown continued to grow up.

A Tour of Ottawa, 1951

I own an official tourist guide to Ottawa from 1951. I bought it, with a smile on my face both at the fact of it and the price, in a book sale. It is 88 pages long, soft-covered and was produced by the city's Industrial and Publicity Bureau. The Bureau used to be at 50 Elgin Street, and the booklet is a combination of adverts and descriptive articles on the delights of Ottawa.

It describes the town as "over a hundred years gradually spreading

over the hills" which makes it sound like a virus—or maple syrup. Produced six years after the end of World War II, the National War Memorial features heavily in the text and in pictures. On the cover, of course, is a graphic of a mounted Mountie with parliament in the background.

This nearing the seventieth anniversary of its publication, and I suppose of the year 1951 itself, I gave the booklet another look. It speaks of another Ottawa, an earlier, shrunken version with a population of a quarter of a million; a whiter, more British Ottawa. Hence the first two adverts in the book are for an English bone china shop and a store selling "finer furs and distinctive apparel for ladies and gentlemen." Next there is an explanation of the city's coat of arms, which carries within it, lest we forget, a rose, a thistle and a shamrock. And no reference to the Algonquin. The civic motto under the coat of arms is "ADVANCE," although there is no mention of how to do that. The mayor's message on page five—it was penned by Grenville Goodwin, who died of a heart attack five months after he wrote it and only nine months after taking office—explains that the city "has been enhanced by planning for a setting of beauty and charm" and he hopes that "sooner or later, most Canadians and many guests from other countries" will come to visit. At Lansdowne Park, the Rough Riders are beginning a season that will take them all the way to victory in the Grey Cup, while the Ottawa Giants baseball team is in a run of home games against Syracuse.

My family emigrated to Canada in 1951, in December, and so it was in the spring of 1952 that we took up Mayor Goodwin's invitation to come and visit and travelled from Belleville in a black 40s Ford to the nation's capital, in fact to scout out a place to live. My father was about to be transferred here, and it was our first glimpse of the city. I was less than a year old, so my memory of the day is nonexistent; I don't recall if we picked

amazon.co.uk

A gift note from Caroline Bowden:

Enjoy your gift of walkies in Ottawa! Stay tuned for delivery of a delightful history of Ottawa in the time of PMs Sir John A MacDonald and Sir Wilfred Laurier, when Ottawa was decidedly NOT the city fun forgot. From Caroline Bowden

Gift note included with **As I Walked About: A Collection of Walking Columns from the Ottawa Citizen**

up an official tourist guide at 50 Elgin or not. Had we done, and turned to page 37, we would have found a sightseeing tour laid out for us. It was while reading this tour and trying to visualize it, that I decided to take it, 1951 Ottawa Tourist Guide (hereafter referred to as the OTG) in hand, and see what had gone and what remained, and to ruminate on what has happened to Ottawa in the intervening decades.

The opening line of the OTG reads "Starting from the National

Unveiling the National War Memorial on Sunday, May 21, 1939.

War Memorial" so that is where I begin. It's that time of day after rush hour and before the sun goes down. The haircuts on the passers-by for the most part could have been worn in the Fifties, but the fashions—tight for the women, loose for the men, with a mixture of suits and shorts thrown in—have advanced. The OTG now directs me to proceed down Wellington between the Langevin Building and the East Block; the street is busy with school kids loading onto buses after a selfie and texting session at the Eternal Flame on the Hill. The streetlamps are festooned with banners illustrating the various provinces and federal institutions; the Parks Canada banner has, as far as I can make out, a deer listening to a folk singer.

Wellington Street, one of the first to be laid out in the city, has come a long way from its early days as a dirt track, a wagon route running up to a British barracks on a promontory with a great overview either side up the river. It has become Canada's Main Street, the place upon which the British consolidated their jurisdiction over the top half of a continent. It was also the northern border of Upper Town, the seat of the moneyed class of Brits and Americans who swarmed in to take advantage of the resource profits the Ottawa valley had to offer.

It is at the corner with Metcalfe that the first change between then and now arrives. Whereas the OTG mentions that here was the Rideau Club, it is now the National Capital Commission's (NCC) Info Centre, already closed for the night, and apparently soon to be vacated. What will appear there next is unknown, but for certain the Rideau Club building was there from 1911 all the way through to 1979, when there was a crippling fire. The sidewall of the building was preserved, but the rest is gone. The Club, founded as a male mover and shaker bastion two years before Confederation, with Sir John A. as its first president, has carried on and gone up in the world. It is now on the fifteenth floor of a Bank Street tower.

The OTG puts the American Embassy next to the Rideau Club, and yes, the building, faced with an attractive Indiana limestone, put up in 1932, is still there, but it is silent and devoid of Americans. The newer, lane-hogging embassy-cum-fortress is over on Sussex, built in 1999. The unused, black doors of the vacant embassy are dirty enough to enjoy some finger-tip graffiti, including a clever one stating *Yankee Move Home*. The hoardings across the front of the building bear a maple leaf motif, a clue to the fact that for a while the former embassy was slated to become the national portrait gallery, till the Harperites down the road in the Langevin building started dissing the notion; that idea too has gone silent. A national portrait gallery with lots of our stuff in it here in the capital makes sense, with sister galleries in each province and territory. But then, what do I know?

The Bank of Montreal is one of Wellington's complement of

self-important stone buildings, limestone at the front and granite towards the lower back, which mimics the local geology quite nicely. It was the last commercial building on the street; the Feds, on our behalf, own it now and everything else on the strip. Eighty years after it was opened the bank sits empty, its most likely, banal fate that of a conference room. The friezes on the exterior are Art Deco depictions of noble workers and buildings joined in the great pursuit of profit-making for the money men.

The OTG mentions that the Norlite Building, which is next as I head west, was the "site of the first theatre house in Ottawa." The Norlite Building houses the waning Press Club now, where once I shared a single malt with Mordecai Richler and we discussed whether the pen was mightier than the snooker cue, but Her Majesty's Theatre was indeed built on the same spot in 1854. It had a decade long run as a theatre, and then it switched to being a publishing house. The old square stone building was replaced by the thin white Norlite Building, built in the Italian Renaissance style, with two pseudo turrets on the façade for spying on members of parliament doing something naughty across the street.

I read in the guide that the old Supreme Court, a low stone building where now there is some sort of vehicular security check, was between the West Block and the Confederation Building. I decide to wander over, and chance upon a couple of interesting things. Firstly, between the Confederation Building and its next door neighbour, the former Justice department, there are large bits of masonry sitting on the grass, a gargoyle or two and some column caps. They appear to have fallen there from the sky, but I suspect, though there is nothing to say what they are, that they are bits left over from the first Parliament Buildings that burnt down in 1916. The other interesting thing is also a piece of masonry. The old Justice Building has its main entrance on the west side, with JUSTICE carved in the stone above and there, perched on the top of the entrance is a kneeling, life-size statue of what would then be called an Indian, with a bow and quiver and an axe. The fact that he is above the word Justice rather than below or to the side of it has an irony that has only appreciated with time. I would have to categorize the look on his face as a scowl.

Forging ahead towards the end of Wellington, I pause for a while outside St. Andrew's Presbyterian Church, which the OTG told visitors in 1951 was the oldest stone church in Ottawa, although the building that is there now was only erected in 1872, well after the Basilica on Sussex. The first church on this site was built by Scottish stonemasons in 1828, and the glebe that went with it, a land grant extended to churches in those days, was later sold and turned into the Glebe with a capital G. I'm normally not a fan of Christian art, much of it focusing on suffering rather than joy, but the depiction of a begging Christ to the left of the doorway, with his punctured outstretched hand, reminds me of the homeless who are always in need of compassion.

Next, at the corner of Wellington and Lyon, the OTG has this to say. I'll quote it in full. "On Lyon Street was located the first market place of Ottawa and to the rear of the old stone building on the corner is the façade of the once splendid residence of Nicholas Sparks, the original owner of all centre town, who purchased 200 acres for $340.00 including a log cabin with furniture. This property today is assessed at over $100,000,000." The rear of Sparks' house was on Wellington, the front on Sparks Street. The house was demolished in 1954, three years after the OTG was published.

In 1951, the year in which we are time travelling, Wellington arced left over to Pooley's Bridge. The OTG suggests looking up on the cliff on the left to take in Christ Church Cathedral with its very pointy side-spire, arched stain-glass frontage and church hall next door. Two separate Church of England high-ups both visited the very young Bytown (later Ottawa) in 1828 and noted in their diaries that while the Catholics, Presbyterians and Methodists already had rudimentary places of worship up and running, the C of E did not. Nicholas Sparks, who had pulled off the trick of getting here four years earlier and buying up land, agreed with them and said they could have a slice of his acreage for the purpose, and before long a large wooden room hosted the first service in July of 1833. At one point the place had to close

Ottawa's history museum, The Bytown.

in the winter because of inadequate heating, but it warmed up and the parishioners gathered for the debut service in the grander building that is there now in September 1874.

Pooley's Bridge, named after a soldier-engineer who worked with Colonel By, is the stone span that crosses the cut of fast-running water separating the "mainland" of Upper Town from LeBreton Flats, which is virtually an island. There has been a bridge of some fashion on this spot for 184 years, although nothing on the bridge itself tells you that. On one side of the bridge is the stately limestone Fleet Street Pumping Station, pumping efficiently since 1875 (a noisy part of town then, what with the cathedral still under construction as well). This was the first piece to be built in the great jigsaw puzzle of Ottawa's water-management system. It removed the need for many of the city's 25,000 residents to buy water at the door from the water salesman, forerunner of the modern, bizarre bottled water craze. If the pumping station ever winds down and comes on the market, it would make a terrific Ottawa Shop, an idea I've been pushing for a while, a place where Ottawa-produced consumables of an artistic nature could be purchased by tourists. The OTG, after mentioning the pumping station as worth a look, directs tourists over Pooley's Bridge and the railway lines of the Canadian Atlantic into what was then the working-class, largely French-Canadian homes and light-industrial businesses of LeBreton Flats. The guide next suggests taking a right onto Duke Street and proceeding over the Chaudière Bridge. You can't get there from here now; Pooley's Bridge is not for cars any more, and Duke Street is gone, as is the neighbourhood of LeBreton Flats, which is in the process of becoming a world-class exhibition site of ugly buildings. So far there is an ugly museum blocking off the river and some hideous condos; the whole thing is turning into a sort of downtown stalag and will no doubt get worse before it gets better, if ever.

Driving down Duke 60 years ago, a capital visitor would pass a tavern, a lumber yard, and at the end of the street a mighty scrap yard, Baker Brothers, run by two orphaned brothers who had fled Ukrainian pogroms in 1901. Tourists in their cars in 1951 could not have known that thirteen years later, in an act of land clearance designed by a French planner and a prime minister's wish to truly capitalize Ottawa, all of LeBreton Flats would be knocked down and sit vacant for close to four decades.

Past the end of Duke Street (said Duke being the Duke of Richmond), the OTG informs us that we will be heading "towards the City of Hull" and that "one may notice the powerful Chaudière Falls which develop some 80,000 horsepower." They have also generated a great deal of history. They were something to portage around on the Native trade route that ran along the Ottawa River more than a millennium ago, and Samuel de Champlain, who also portaged around them in the June of 1613, wrote in his notebook, "this waterfall makes such a noise in this basin that it can be heard for more than two leagues away." Champlain also described the land that would later become Ottawa as "nothing more than rough, steep rocks, covered with poor scrubby wood."

With the coming of industry after 1800, the Falls were quickly tamed and hooked up to the business of making money for such entrepreneurs as E. B. Eddy. It is to be hoped that sixty years hence the Falls are once again open to the public, perhaps in a park linking the historic lower and upper Canadas. But for now, standing on the Chaudière Bridge, I am mesmerized by the tamed, pinched foaming power of the Chaudière Falls. The OTG states that "the industry located either side of the bridge is the E. B. Eddy company, paper manufacturers." (Ezra Butler Eddy, an American from Vermont, got here in 1854 and started out making sulphur matches by hand in a shed near the Chaudière. In 1886 he shifted from lighting paper to making it and made a fortune.)

The guide then urges us to be "turning left and driving along Route No. 8 to the Royal Ottawa Golf Club, turn left and cross the Ottawa River again over the Champlain Bridge." That is the scant mention the city then called Hull and its founders get in the booklet. Perhaps the guide's author, knowing that many of the tourists using it would be Americans—the inside back page of the OTG is devoted to an ad for the Prescott-Ogdensburg ferry—would not dwell long in what would appear to them almost a foreign country, where ils ne parlent pas American.

This cursory mention of Hull, which predates Ottawa, is to my mind a gap in the OTG; had I been its author I would have informed the visitor that its founder Philemon Wright, after three visits to the area in the late 1790s, came up the frozen river in late winter 1800 and planted himself and his followers on the north side of the Chaudière in 1800. Ironically, he was led there by an Algonquin guide, a case of the deer leading the wolf in. Wright sent the area's first timber raft down the river in 1806, his town survived a settlement-destroying fire in 1808, and he died in 1839, almost eighty; he is buried in St. James Anglican cemetery. The population of Hull in 1951 was 50,000, half that of Ottawa, and the waterfront was a working one.

The Route No. 8 the OTG mentions, now Taché Boulevard, is today a conveyor belt for cars, built up on either side with only the occasional stretch of open ground. Firstly, there is the unkempt, vacant 1892 E.B. Eddy warehouse, which would make a terrific arts centre or concert hall. On the other side is an aqueduct, with the Théâtre de l'Île, a converted aqueduct building, in midstream. Nearby on the same side, set back, is the former Wright residence, built by Wright's grandson when the original burnt down and now owned by the NCC and rented out as apartments. A little further along, on the corner of St-Joseph is the Salaberry Armoury, younger than it looks, having been built the year World War II broke out. The several tanks in front are a giveaway. Salaberry was a Quebecer who fought for the Brits in the War of 1812. Turn right past there and the 1951 visitors could take a side trip into Gatineau Park, created in 1938, or turn left on Bégin and visit the stonefaced statue of black-robed Father Jean de Brébeuf, erected in 1926, three hundred years after he paddled through here, not as a tourist but as a seeker of souls.

Staying on Route No. 8, several miles along on the right is the Moore Farm Estate, a virtually intact agricultural oasis which goes back 150 years, then the stately beginnings of the Royal Ottawa Golf Club; I'd be surprised if any royal has ever played there. Then quickly into the left-hand lane to get onto the Champlain Bridge, our longest bridge which crosses a trio of islands: Bate, Cunningham and Riopelle.

No sightseeing tour of any city is complete without a drift through some of the finer real estate, made in a seesawing state of envy and disparagement. The guide is happy to tell us that "following Island Park Drive you will see many beautiful homes and also pass the residences of the Mexican and Peruvian Ambassadors to Canada." I wonder how people can afford these places; clearly they are not columnists. The OTG suggests we follow Island Park until it reaches the tranquil acres of the Experimental Farm.

The Experimental Farm is boxed in now, but back then it was out on the rural border of Ottawa, though the city had recently quadrupled in size after an amalgamation. In 1951 the Farm's director, Mr. Edgar S. Archibald, had just retired after thirty-one years and the Arboretum—for me the natural heart of the city that must remain development-free until the day after Armageddon—is listed in the guide as a must-see, not least for its garden of medicinal plants.

A windows down, elbows out drive along the canal is

recommended next, on the west side; the east side ends in railway tracks. Our tourists do not pass under the Queensway, still a decade away from being flown over the driveway, instead they turn left at Laurier and continue along the canal and past the Roxborough apartments and arrive at the War Memorial again, where we started. Passing between the Grand Trunk's monumental Union Station, then in its heyday, and the Loire Valley-esque copper spires of the Chateau Laurier, the guide directs us left across the streetcar tracks onto Sussex, with government workers entering and leaving the venerable Daly building, though none are lingering outside to smoke, something they are perfectly able to do indoors.

Rewinding through that previous paragraph with modern eyes, we can note that the Daly building is gone, shamefully replaced with a concrete cube by a National Capital Commission that is nowadays much occupied with building luxury condominiums for all Canadians. The streetcars quit the streets in 1959, the Chateau Laurier is again owned by Canadians and a train hasn't pulled into Union Station since 1966.

Our motoring run down 1951 Sussex as far as St. Patrick allows us to peruse the OLD STONE BUILDINGS, as the OTG refers to them, at least on the east side. In 1951, many of these stoners were privately owned and not as spruced up as they are now. The largely successful NCC campaign to purchase and restore them did not begin until 1961, a campaign that included the conversion of an unoccupied warehouse into the famous Le Hibou coffee house. It has resulted in the slightly high-rent model-village feel the east side has in the Byward Market section.

The west side of Sussex now has a mere three buildings, only one of which was there in 1951, the rear of the Connaught Building, which opened in 1916 and was originally used as a customs examining warehouse, which sounds more intriguing than it probably was. (If you recognize the Connaught's style of architecture, it's because the gentleman who designed it, David Ewart, also drew up the plans for the Museum of Nature and the Royal Mint.) Where Fort American Embassy is now was a temporary government building in 1951, a hangover from the Second World War that lasted until 1972. The OTG insists on a detour leftwards down to Nepean Point, then reachable without leaving the car. To get there one drove past the large square Government Printing Bureau, which sat about where the National Gallery is now. Having got us to Nepean Point the guide makes no mention of Champlain's statue with its upside down astrolabe, but instead informs us that, "The "Frontier Post" marks the Canadian-American frontier at the 45 degree parallel of latitude, between New York State and the Province of Quebec, in virtue of the Washington Treaty of 1842." Although I've been to Nepean Point many a time, I cannot recall seeing this post. But with my OTG I found it, just to the right of the statue, a waist-high bronze obelisk, put there by our Women's Historical Society. The post was donated to Ottawa in 1902 when the original border markers were replaced by granite ones. It now marks the spot where the border exactly isn't.

The view from Nepean Point in 1951 was of an Ottawa that was, well, lower, less high-risey, more stolid and solid, with plumes of steam engine smoke rising here and there, and perhaps a train itself on the tracks below running by the canal locks. The backdrop to the buildings on Wellington was clear sky, not filled

Looking east from Nepean Point, 1949. Royal Mint centre right.

with the intrusive thrusts of banks and exchange centres. It was a more European view. Sixty years on, the rise of the car and the rise in architecture have made it distinctly North American.

Coming down from Nepean Point and sending me along Sussex, the OTG mentions Laurentian Terrace, at number 360. After some considerable searching I found this reference to it in a footnote, in a book about Mennonites. "The Laurentian Terrace, a very large and rambling two storey wooden structure, is the best known example of the quarters provided by the government for unmarried girls working in wartime Ottawa. That facility continued in operation until the mid-1960s." Hopefully, several women reading this will be recalling their time behind those wooden walls.

Across the street, the La Salle Academy was also involved, in a Catholic sort of way, in the welfare of young people. A fine building, it started out, in 1852, three years before Ottawa became a city, as Bytown College, but that only lasted for four years. After that it was rented out and became a hotel. (The college leapfrogged across town and grew into the University of Ottawa.) In 1866 it was co-opted as a barracks and did that for another four-year stint before reverting back to a school. Then, in 1879, the property was bought by Les Frères des Écoles Chrétiennes, the Christian Brothers, who converted it into a dual business and science school, and it mostly stayed in the education game from 1899 to 1970 as the Académie De La Salle, which lives on in various alumni websites. I say mostly, because in October 1949, the Canadian Repertory Theatre company, who had moved in, put on their inaugural play there. The play, appropriately for Ottawa back then, was called *Quiet Weekend*. The Company lasted four years before moving to its present home in Stratford, but in those brief months illuminati such as Christopher Plummer, Amelia Hall, William Shatner and William Hutt trod the boards there.

As with many other buildings in Ottawa, the academy was trapped in the federal web in 1970, and remains so, functioning as, according to the small sign on the door, the Canada School of Public Service. Clearly, with a name like that, this is a front for a black-ops operation. The academy has a smaller building attached to it, at one time the bishop's home, and there is a really rather pleasant lunching park at the rear, with a great, à propos figurative sculpture of marching civil servants in the middle that brings a smile to my face. It's by William McElcheran. Next door, the Grey Nuns have their convent, cornering the Elizabeth Bruyère Centre, formerly the general hospital, with its several splendid art deco doors.

Hopping back across the street, the OTG lays out the run of edifices that incorporated the Canadian War Museum, the Public Archives and the Royal Mint. There is a stone embedded in the wall of the building that signifies that an extension was built to the Archives in 1925, and many war artifacts were housed within. When the archives shifted over to the present building on Wellington in 1967, the War Museum occupied the entire space, all the way up to 2004 when the new one opened on the Flats. Apparently the building now hosts the Aga Khan's Global Centre for Pluralism, whatever that may mean, but the building was singularly lifeless when I walked across the forecourt up to the front door. In doing so I stepped on a flagstone reminding me that this was once the General Motors Court. Yes, for several years the Canadian War Museum was "sponsored" by an American car company who stuck their name all over it. How Monty Python is that? The Royal Mint has been minting it since 1908, when Lord and Lady Grey activated the presses.

"Further along Sussex on the right the visitor passes the FIRST RAILWAY STATION in Bytown; on the extreme left may be seen EARNSCLIFFE, residence of British High Commissioners to Canada." The OTG is casual in its mention of our premier railway station, which stood, in various incarnations, roughly where the Saudi Embassy is now. A station was there until 1960, when it burnt down, and a little later the track was removed. There is a first class documentary waiting to be made about Ottawa's railway history, perhaps as a series on the radio. As for Earnscliffe, built in 1855 by Thomas McKay for his son-in-law, these days it may *not* be seen; the gates are designed to exclude gawking, likewise the blacked-out fence that guards the perimeter. Somewhere in there Commissioners are busy commissing, as they have done since 1930, when the Brits bought it from the last of a series of well-to-do gentlemen who had lived there and enjoyed the view, including Prime Minister John A. Macdonald. Our first PM died there on a Saturday evening in the June of 1891, and his body travelled from the nearby Sussex train station to Kingston for burial.

I have never been inside the Herzberg Building, the National Research Council's original headquarters built at 100 Sussex in 1930. I never fail to admire its classical bulk when I pass it, as does the OTG. It was dubbed the "Temple of Science" when it opened and the name fits. Gerhard Herzberg, whose name the building proudly carries, was working and directing there in 1951 on his way to a Nobel prize in chemistry. I peek through the doors and catch a glimpse of a security guard seated beneath a chandelier flanked by two gorgeous marble staircases. My father, an electronic engineer, had business there many a time, and I'm sure there are all sorts of wondrous things still going on within its ornate limestone, granite and sandstone walls, including biohazard research.

When you are fashioning twin cities at a point on the map where three rivers meet up, you are going to have to build a lot of bridges. The Rideau River has to fall down a fair height to mingle with the Ottawa, and because it has a lump in its mouth, Green Island, it bifurcates and goes either side. That is why there are two bridges over the Rideau on Sussex Drive. They are called the Bytown Bridges; their first incarnation was in 1846, and they got a serious makeover about a decade ago.

Walking the stretch between the first Bytown Bridge and the gates of Rideau Hall, with the OTG open at page 41, I am informed that the Rideau Falls have a perpendicular drop of 37 feet. This is how far the ice chunks have to fall when they blast open the river in spring, and as far as I know no one has ever unwittingly tumbled those 37. Upriver, the Chaudière has claimed more than one victim, including Benjamin Moore in 1815 and James Hawley in 1836 but there are no tales of Rideau river riders.

The OTG informs me that, "On Green Island are the buildings of the Federal Bureau of Statistics. Canada took the first nominal census in the world in 1666. Across the second bridge and on your left is the National Film Board, next to the French Embassy and beyond is the residence of the Prime Minister of Canada." The used-to-be our town hall sits now on Green Island, and from the outside it appears curiously un-busy, compared to the days when it hosted council meetings and the payment of parking fines. The Green Island building wasn't there in 1951, and neither was City Hall in any form. From 1931 until 1958, Ottawa was run from several upper floors of the elegant Transportation Building on Rideau, which is still there, sticking up like a healthy thumb, on the north-west corner of the Rideau Centre. The civic administration was hurriedly bunged in there when the City Hall on Elgin burnt down in 1931. When the international style hall opened for argument—in August, 1958—it claimed to be the first building in Ottawa to be air-conditioned. Imagine a city without cool air, without all those interior oases we take for granted now.

The guide is sort of correct in mentioning Canada's first census. Actually, it was gathered in New France, and it was conducted personally by the Intendant of the colony at the time, Jean Talon, on horseback rather than online. He didn't include the Natives, and arrived at a total of 3215, or a full house in the Opera of the National Arts Centre. On the NFB's website there are several 50s video tours of Ottawa, including one from 1957. They are definitely from another era, and all the more interesting, and chuckle inducing, because of that.

The open ground where the Film Board building once was, next to the fabulous, Art Deco 1939 French Embassy, with a room entirely panelled in birch bark, is dotted with various monuments to Canadians who have fallen in belligerent or compassionate service abroad. Nearby sits the vacant NCC building with rusty railings, the once upon a time "Canada and the World" pavilion. According to the NCC it was a "great success," and so they shut it down.

Depending on who is in residence, I either flick a bird or give a thumbs-up as I drive or walk past 24 Sussex. In 1951

Prime Minister St-Laurent had only just moved in, reluctantly. St-Laurent, along with many other federal politicians, was happy as a bug in a bed in a bachelor flat in the Roxborough Apartments on Elgin, and only moved onto Sussex on the condition that he pay rent, which subsequent PMs did until 1971. 24 Sussex started out as a private home, built by Joseph Currier, an American who came to town in 1837 aged a mere seventeen, and, as was the fashion, made a fortune in lumber. He called his new home, which he moved into in 1868 with his third wife, "Gorffwysfa," which is Welsh for "place of peace." By then Currier had lost four children and two wives, the second dying within two months of the wedding, so his naming of his home was a hopeful one. The Federal government went after the building in 1943, serving an expropriation notice on the then owner, another lumber baron, W.C. Edwards. Edwards fought back, and then died, so the government won, and St-Laurent hung his hat there.

After stopping to chat with the man from the NCC in shorts painting the railings black, and peering into the windows of the cute, small stone building on the corner of the 24 Sussex grounds, which carries the number 10, and noting the very large TV screen within showing cartoons, I scurry across the end of Sussex at the nicely landscaped roundabout and amble up to the gates of Rideau Hall. A young man in a red tunic, large fur hat on his head, is inertly on guard while he has his photograph taken with a barely dressed tourist. I give him my sympathies and settle for a while under a shady bough in the grounds of Thomas McKay's old place, where, in 1951, a young princess called Elizabeth planted a tree.

The OTG is correct in saying the stone and red tile lookout in Rockcliffe Park provides "a glorious one hundred and eighty degree vista" of rivers and rumpled land. Champlain came past here in June, 1613, and perhaps looked up from his canoe at the spot where I'm standing. It's a view that has fattened up since 1951 but is still thick with trees. The OTG suggests that directly opposite the lookout one might see a log boom being made ready for shunting over to E. B. Eddy's. No chance of seeing that today. What I can also see now are the towers of the electronic age, blinking away in the Gatineau Hills. The very air itself is so much fuller now of conversation and image and music.

No sightseeing tour would let us leave Rockcliffe without rubbernecking the "exclusive residential area." I dutifully head down Acacia, past "the home of the Leader of the Progressive Conservative Party." The George Drew family would have been living there in 1951. The OTG leads me onto Buena Vista, which as its name implies does provide a pleasant view, mansions, embassies and the like, then past Elmwood girl's school, which retails a better class of education and was founded in 1915 by a teacher with the gloriously Wildean name of Theodora Philpot. Over the site of the old street car tracks, then back to Sussex and down MacKay, where the majority of houses are now brick, not stone, and to the intersection with Beechwood. Turning right, we would have passed the Linden movie house on the corner with Crichton, where *Singing in the Rain* might well have been playing, over the St. Patrick Street bridge (which could enjoy a little beautification like its southern neighbour, the Cummings Bridge) and then I am directed to turn down Wurtemburg, which one could in 1951 but would cause an accident if you tried it now, as it is sealed off. The Chinese Embassy used to be on Wurtemburg—it's in a converted convent these days on St. Patrick, which is nicely ironic—and China was only a year into the Maoist revolution in 1951.

The open space of Strathcona Park as I turn onto Laurier comes as a relief after all that real estating, and I sigh with pleasure as I circumnavigate Lord Strathcona's classic, lovely fountain and pass a reviving half hour watching stress-reduced human beings of all shapes and sizes play in pools, stroll along the Rideau or bench themselves much as they would have done six decades ago. The park is reclaimed swamp, as are other parts of Ottawa. It started out as a rifle range and, after it became a park in the first decade of the 20th century, contained the city's first golf course.

I have to confess, in forty years of living here, I had never set foot in Laurier House. With more than adequate reason now, I pay the peculiar yet small entrance fee of $3.90 and am very well-guided through three floors of antiques and prime ministerial

Strathcona Park postcard from its glory days.

goings on. Both Wilfrid Laurier and Mackenzie King died in this home; indeed, King had only been dead a year when the OTG was published. At one point the guide opened the door to a cupboard full of air ducts and what have you, and told us that in its day this had been King's gloomy, bare-bones séance salon. I scanned the space mentally but heard neither a voice nor a bark. The third floor was the most intriguing, and I would happily move into the library, from which King, a bachelor homebody at heart, ran the country whenever he could; Churchill and Roosevelt discussed war strategies here. The highlight of the tour for me was in King's bedroom, where he had a life-mask of the face and hands of Abraham Lincoln. Now that is history.

I park the car and walk from Laurier House to the War Memorial, to the starting point of the tour. A piper is blaring away on the grass in front of Tabaret Hall (constructed in 1905 and modeled on Washington's Capitol Building) causing the Ottawa University students around him to turn up their mp3s and shout louder into their cell phones. Ottawa must have been a quieter place in the Fifties. At the War Memorial, amid all the people of the present tense scurrying to and fro, an older woman stands still in front of it, head bowed.

The Outer Limits

Manotick Main Street, 1927.

A few months ago the City of Ottawa put out an official boundary map of itself that can be purchased in cartography stores. Map shops offer you the world and are always worth a visit, so I visit my favourite map emporium and buy a map of all Ottawa for a mere twenty bucks.

The map, like Ottawa itself, is big and flat. According to the City's website, post-2001 amalgamation Ottawa covers an area half the size of Prince Edward Island, which if you haven't been to Prince Edward Island means nothing. Let me use the great Canadian area analogy instead, and you'll grasp it right away. Ottawa is the size of 342,190 CFL football fields. (I was going to work it out in hockey rinks, but let's not go there.) The map is half the dimensions of a king-sized sheet. Laying it out on the floor, I notice that the city boundaries carve out the rough shape of a cut diamond, the kind that would be set into a ring. The notion of visiting the three corners of Ottawa perked my sense of adventure and I gave the map closer scrutiny. This journey in three acts will take me upriver almost to Arnprior; a little ways past Cumberland downriver, and a goodly ways south to a set of locks of the Rideau Canal.

Heading, like a good voyageur, westwards I try as much as possible to parallel the river. This takes me through the village of Constance Bay, named after Simon Constant, the Algonquin who was supplanted by cottagers and full-time residents. (One such cottager, a Mr. Watson, went a-digging in his yard in the 1970s and unearthed a ceramic pot that was fashioned when the Pharaohs of Egypt began their dynasty.)

Passing through Fitzroy Park and over the Mississippi, I chase my own tailpipe like a dog along a fenced-in stretch of railway line until I get myself on Route 29 and as close as I can to Lake Madawaska. Getting out on foot I walk down a muddy road to water's edge and stand by a hunter's unoccupied wetland hide. The water tower on the edge of Arnprior is visible in the distance. A swim and a short hike in a meadow would take me to Ottawa's westerly tip, but I pass on that level of journalistic integrity, and am content to have witnessed it.

Driving back through Ottawa and out the other side, I take the Rockcliffe Parkway and stay on the old river road, past Petrie Island (which gratefully received its annual clean up of litter left by the litter scum this last weekend) and that lovely short stretch that boasts the wide river on the driver's side and interesting cliffs on the passenger's wing. A tight turn takes me up to the well-kept, unflustered Cumberland main street, which, it being a Sunday, is populated only by a barking dog and a bored young man watching a movie in the general store. Back on the highway I travel just past the junction with the Canaan Road and there is the "You Are Entering Ottawa" sign. Crossing a field for sale, I reach the river's edge. This time, instead of a hunter's hide, I find myself next to a bright blue ice fishing hut.

The best way to reach the southern tip of Ottawa is to roll down the Dwyer Hill Road, past signs for Lord-of-the-Rings sounding places like Munster Hamlet and Malakoff, and to come out at Burritt's Rapids at the locks, a fine place to have a picnic. Turn right on Highway 2, go a short way along and there is the "Welcome/Bienvenue to Ottawa" sign on the south side of the road, pointing towards some wetlands again. The latest population figure, printed on a piece of plastic paper and stuck over the old number, reads 900,000. A short detour into the neighbouring county takes me into Andrewsville, founded in 1843 by the Andrews brothers, and which once reached a population of 200, where they are fighting to keep their trestle bridge. It is still there.

Making the three-corner expedition around Ottawa's boundaries has altered my way of seeing the city. It is a vast field edged and bisected by water, with a city in it bunched up at the top, not a city surrounded by ruralism. Geographically, rather than demographically, it would make more sense for the town hall to be in Manotick or Richmond, which isn't going to happen, but as the fields rapaciously turn to suburbs you realize that greater Ottawa is not made of two solitudes, but it is bipolar, with acres of quietude impregnated with grids of noise. And it's getting noisier by the year.

Ashton Station Road

One of the several log homes on Ashton Station Road.

*T*here is an official turtle crossing just outside the Ashton United Church. It operates from May through to September, and this being late August, I'm waiting to see if a snapper or two makes a crawl—look left, look right—for the other side of Ashton Station Road. The Jock River is down beside the church and after the memorable summer we've had, it's dry as bone, so maybe the turtles are jaywalking elsewhere.

Since the 2001 amalgamation, Ashton Station Road forms part of the south-western boundary line for Ottawa. Thus Flewellyn Road, which runs perpendicular to the Station Road, and which I am about to walk down, is in Ottawa, while the church is in Beckwith Township. Flewellyn Road (clearly named for a Welsh settler) is the historic heart of Ashton, and from here seems to be inhabited by alternating churches and log homes.

The blue City of Ottawa Ashton sign states that the village was settled in 1851, and that settler was John Sumner. The site Sumner chose was near the headwaters of the Goodwood River, which gave the nascent village the hydraulic power it needed— and every small Ontario town needed—to establish a mill. As the village attracted more settlers, Sumner became the postmaster. A mere fifteen years after Sumner put down roots here, the village had reached a three figure population, had a couple of stone churches reflecting the religious tribal affiliations of its immigrants, a school, and the river had been renamed the Jock, after a Frenchman named Jacques had drowned in it. (Sadly, there is a plaque on the Jock River bridge attesting to the drowning of a young girl in 1998. "May this river never claim another life" is etched on the plaque. Indeed.)

The stone Ashton general store, the first building on my right, is sadly vacant at the moment, but it has been recently purchased and will come to life once more as a general merchants, although without a post office within, or so I am told by the new owner. Like the general store in Pakenham, which has managed to retain its bygone-days character, entering the store in Ashton was like stepping back in time. Hopefully its new management will likewise create an emporium blending past and present.

By the time I reach the community notice board on the south side of Flewellyn, past the cemetery, I've seen or glimpsed through foliage more grey log and mortar-chinked homes and barns per half mile than I've seen anywhere else in Ottawa. Along the way there is the inevitable cluttered building devoted to the internal combustion engine, some excellent gardening, as well as an active stone church and nearby a passive one. The bank of super mailboxes at the entrance to the community centre looks as though it has arrived from the future, which at one time it did. Someone should do a photo book of community notice boards; they are a portrait of a community's character.

Arriving back again at the United Church steps, I make a small detour south and cross the bridge over the Jock River. Readers looking for a walk down a country lane can pick up the long McCaffrey Trail here on the corner of the bridge. On the other side a large sign in a field announces that a housing development, Ashton Heights, will be arriving soon. Its billboard wants potential modern settlers to know that there will be fibre optics, Hydro, and WiFi.

Despite the walk being rather brief, there is need for refreshment in the revitalized Old Mill at Ashton pub, which is now the reason most non-Ashtonians head there. As I take a sip of stout brewed on the premises, I recall a friend who was a member of the Ottawa Valley Hunt saying that this was their watering hole. Indeed the Hunt's mailing address is listed as being in Ashton, and the history blurb on its website reveals that it is "one of the oldest foxhunting organizations on the continent" and that its founder, in 1873, was Lord Dufferin, who was Governor General at the time. A line of horses outside the pub would look just about right in Ashton.

Avon Lane

Looking north down the beauty of Avon Lane.

The immaculately timed arrival of summer on the weekend of the solstice encouraged me to put on my strolling sandals and head for a walk I have had on my list ever since I lived in New Edinburgh in the early 1980s. The neighbourhood's streets were well established and groomed, the pre-condo domestic architecture a pleasure to walk past, with plenty of detail for the eye to savour and appreciate. And then there were the lanes, the narrow pathways running between the back gardens of houses on two parallel streets. I would glimpse them as I passed by porches and gentrified homes, but never got around to exploring them.

So now I would walk the longer of the two lanes, Avon. (The other is River Lane.) The lanes were part of Thomas MacKay's original grid for New Edinburgh, laid out shortly after he bought a whack of land in 1829 south of the Ottawa River and east of the still in construction Rideau Canal—and I have walked similar lanes in Edinburgh, Scotland, his home town, and enjoyed romantic teenage liaisons in the back alleys of Liverpool. They add to the charm of the district, and Avon Lane gave me as rewarding a walk as any other I've done in the past.

I start at the southern end of the Lane, which is on Dufferin (Frederick Blackwood, Lord Dufferin, was governor general of Canada from 1872 to 1878) halfway between MacKay to the east and Crichton (MacKay's wife's maiden name) to the west. It is easy to imagine the lane when it was unpaved, and minus the storm gutter along the side, a horse and carriage delivering a father home after a day's merchanting or civil servicing in Bytown. This daydream is diluted somewhat by the forest of leaning poles of the electrical grid and the fact that it is garbage day, plastic bins and outcast stuff clumped at the lane's edge.

On my right as I take my first steps into the lane is the side of MacKay United Church, built in the arts and crafts style beginning in 1909. The rear of the School of Dance comes up quickly on my left, a building I remember fondly from when it was the city archives, and where I spent hours rooting around in Ottawa's history. The landscape, to my left and right, now alternates between garages and backyard fences and graveled parking lots. Little pocket-sized gardens find space where they can, and the abundance of trees gives the lane an air of human co-habitation with nature, rather than overwhelming it as so often happens now on our thoroughfares.

Crossing first Keefer (MacKay's son-in-law), then Union, I come to a particularly pretty stretch where the houses face into the lane rather than showing their backs. I hope the Ottawa Film Office is aware of these houses in the Avon Lane low numbers; the location register should include them. By now I am an expert in garage architecture, from the veterans with weak hips slowly falling over to the modern glass and stained wood, from the basketball hoops above the doors to wooden sheds stuffed with the overflow of consumerism.

The end of the lane comes too soon, despite my turtle pace, and frequent bloom-sniffing stops, when I am confronted with a dam in the flow consisting of garages on the north side of School Lane. (Avon has an orphaned section the other side of the garages, running between Charles and Thomas, two of MacKay's sons.) Turning 180 degrees, I walk back, my mood elevated as it always is by urban pockets of beauty and eccentricity.

On a less charming note, as I drive away from New Edinburgh along Beechwood, I am forced to behold, after such a pleasant stroll, the construction site of the condos that are replacing the row of interesting and eclectic stores lost in the fire in March, 2011. The New Edinburgh pub, where I made music with friends many a time, is in mid-demolition. Pity.

Bank Street

The Bank Street Bridge, 1916. Restored in 1993.

*T*he correct place to start a comprehensive walk down Bank Street is on the bank of the Ottawa River, which is how the street got its name. I can't see north across the river to the governmental towers of Gatineau—today is the year's first snowstorm, and a mighty one at that—but I can just make out the pewtery water ahead.

Trudging across Lover's Walk, I ascend the limestone cliff by a cold metal staircase coming into a car park, head up another winding wooden staircase into another car park, and here is the beginning of modern Bank Street, which if you look all the way down it from this vantage, eventually turns into Highway 31 and goes all the way to the St. Lawrence, linking the two watery transport routes of old.

When I get to the corner of Bank and Wellington, the sign says I'm actually at number 57 Bank, an address that has long disappeared as a household. Bank was the first street in Uppertown to push south from the river, getting a head start after Nicholas Sparks subdivided a portion of his farm in 1826. Sparks, a canny fellow, pulled off the Canadian colonial trick of getting here early and snapping up a whack of un-ceded land and then flipping it. The streetcar began riding the rails southward down Bank in 1891, pulling the city limits along with it.

On the south side, I pop into the foyer of the elegant limestone-dressed House of Commons administration building, partly to de-ice my wings. Looking up into the vaulted ceiling I behold a seriously large mosaic, with noble sentiments spelt out and floating ladies in white billowy dresses. This is the old Met Life insurance building, built 1927, and the mosaic is by an American, Barry Faulkner. This stepping into governmental foyers and catching a nice architectural oddity is getting to be a habit. Last time I did it I bumped into a piece of the Berlin wall.

On the other side of Bank is a forlorn elevated stone plaza, decorated with a statue of a mechanistic Icarus called *Flight*, by Yol. The piece was imported from the Canada Pavilion at Expo '67 to here. I wonder if it would work to encase this plaza, which is dead space in the winter, and greenhouse it. Actually, a network of greenhouse coffee/tea shops across the city that only emerge in the frozen months would be a fine treat to give ourselves.

The shoebox high rise next to the plaza bears one of those black signs with white lettering that tell you this is a government stockade; in this case the C. D. Howe building. The sign also indicates that you are about to pass an architectural black hole. It's been downhill in this town for government buildings ever since the splendid Langevin Block at the top of Elgin rose up in 1884.

Things are better on the other side of the road, where within a block of the Sparks Street Mall there is a streamlined building and a little Art Deco gem at the corner of Slater. The pastel grey streamlined building is now a jeweler, and there's a coffee shop in the Art Deco example. (I'm a fan of the strict elegance of Deco, and I'm in the wrong town for it; we have a meagre stock, although Barry Hobin and Charlesfort have just added to it wonderfully with the Hudson Park apartment block on Kent. Havana, Cuba is Deco mecca.) The Ottawa Hydro Commission commissioned the Deco architect W. C. Beattie to build it in 1934 and it has so far survived redevelopment and merited a Heritage plaque.

As I move south, Bank Street is a potpourri of strips of two- and three-storey red-bricks on both sides, painted or au naturel, broken up by the ubiquitous invasion of cold glass façades, including a totally banal new Shopper's Drug Mart that has no right being downtown, but I doubt anyone at Town Hall was prepared to hold up a flat palm and ask them to rethink it. Which is a shame, because it runs counter to the streetscape facelift that has just been completed and runs down to Gladstone. You'll notice it most in the square grey matt metal bike racks and waste basket holders. Look closer at the bike racks and you'll see that the central panel design is nifty. The City commissioned twenty-seven local artists to come up with thirty designs and they did. You can see them all together on the City's website, under Bank Street rehabilitation. Collect all thirty on your promenades between Laurier and the Queensway.

On the west side, just before the Beaux-Art bank at number 186 that surely has the most elegant wheelchair ramp in the city, there is a rare empty space with a brick flower bed and a single small tree in the middle; it has a slightly Japanese style to it. A low railing fence and two gates, both padlocked. This vacant space is actually a testament to the big bang that occurred here in 1958.

On October 25th of that year, a gas leak joined up with a spark and flattened several buildings on Slater, put twenty people in the Civic Hospital. The blast also took out a third of the Odeon Cinema, another Art Deco offering which had been open less than a decade and stood at 142 Bank. It seated 1500 people; fortunately the explosion came in the morning.

As I canter through the Stygian Queensway underpass on Bank Street, resuming my walk and talk where it left off at Gladstone, I'm sure these things must score below zero on the Jane Jacob's walkability scale. Is there anything uglier than an underpass? Must they be so darn crass, or could someone out there, a Carleton architecture student perhaps, come up with a cheap, neat way of brightening them. Maybe some curves and barn board and a couple of flat screens showing Canadian art?

But for now there it is in all its tediousness, the gateway to the Glebe, the St. Andrew's church lands conceded well over a century ago to the homebuilders and developers. I once suffered, at a GCTC musical concert, through a rant by a particularly testosterone-filled, out-of-town alt-country songwriter. He was sticking it to the Glebe, with which he had only passing acquaintance, with evident relish, thereby increasing, or so he thought, his cool rating. Out came all the clichés in an adjectival string—CBC listening, natural-fibre wearing, organics hugging, NDP voting, free-range-kid having, maxed-out-library-card holding, PhD waving. There were many Glebites in the room that night, and no one fought back, but I remember thinking, even if what you say is partly true, what exactly is wrong with that? I've never lived in the Glebe but I've spent a fair bit of time there and drunk a lot of their beer and coffee, and I have a fondness for the community. Try saying that about Barrhaven.

Standing (briefly) in the middle of the road by the Clocktower brew pub and looking down the asphalt flatness of the stretch of Bank between the overpass (c.1965) and the delightfully retro-fitted Bank Street Bridge (1912), one first beholds an almost unbroken ribbon of retail, save for a church here and there. Then the absence of trees becomes apparent (not good), and the likewise absence of high-rise buildings (good).

Setting off, and walking in turn past a sewing emporium, an alternative music store, a weird I'm-not-quite-sure-what shop, then a beauty store then an animal hospital, the eclectic retail adventure that is the Glebe begins. With the odd franchise exception, the rest of the walk will entail going past owner-run stores where one emerges either with something in a bag, or in one's stomach. (Sorry to do this again, but is there anyone at City Hall capable of rapping Shopper's Drug Mart's knuckles and getting them to at least try to fit in architecturally? There is a McDonald's in Siena that could almost pass for an art gallery café, because they were told to do it that way.)

There is a brief stutter after that short burst of retail, on both sides, with the Chinese United Church at 600 followed by the Ambassador Court apartments, built to a Noffke design, the architect who, along with David Younghusband, built quite a few of the Glebe's better houses. Then the bridge over Central Park, the park looking delightful and underused in the snow. The stairway down into the park is blocked but the closure has been duly ignored by tobogganers who know a good slide when they see one. Just over the bridge I pass an empty lot on the east side. Several hostelries including the pretty Grove Hotel (1873) once stood here, at the streetcar stop for Electric Park on the edge of town, which had a bandstand and a water theme and is long gone.

And so it goes until I reach the avenues, First to Fifth, the heart of the matter. It begins with Dr. McElroy's 1910 home, which sits like a silk cravat at the northeast corner of First Avenue, and which is now a seller of fine men's clothing, the other end of the scale from the St. Vincent de Paul that I sartorially frequent.

Between First and Second on the west side here stood the Avalon movie house, the first in Ottawa to show the miracle of film with sound. It lasted from 1928 until 1954, an early casualty in Ottawa's dwindling stock of stand-alone movie houses. In the supermarket nearby, in a corner of the window, the local historical society has a display board up, facing inwards, with delightful photographs of a family's decade-long tenure on First

Avenue, a reminder that we all have neighbours from the past as well as the present. On the sidewalk outside the supermarket is the Glebe's one and only begging point, which seems to run seven days a week. Luckily I find a toonie in my pocket and drop it on the gentleman's cardboard carpet.

Moving southward, there are occasional rewards for looking across the street and up to the second stories rather than gazing into the shop windows. One of the earliest residences on the east side of Bank Street, built in 1878, the Dewar house, is actually still there, but it's hidden behind and slightly above the Body Shop at number 797. It's a tiny survivor, a fine setting for a short story by one of the Glebe's band of writers.

There is a slight commercial mood shift south of Fifth, with the welcome conviviality of Irene's Pub and a booze shop, and then it all comes to an end, and here is a senior's residence compound on one side and Lansdowne Park on the other. It was Lansdowne Park that the streetcar line was making for when it opened in 1891, and accounts for the ruler straightness of Bank. Here and now is not the place to get into a discussion of Lansdowne, a work-in-progress (or regress depending how far back you go). There will be ample opportunity elsewhere in the years to come.

Look closely in among the mishmash of seniors' housing styles opposite Lansdowne and you'll discover the 1867 Alexander Mutchmor House, called Abbotsford after the birthplace of the writer Sir Walter Scott. It gets the blue ribbon for Best House on Street, and if you stare into the front room window you'll see a large photograph of elephants parading through Ottawa. I spoke once at Mutchmor House and Janet, who was in the audience, explained the elephant picture. "I grew up in the Glebe, and as a little girl I remember going with my father to watch the Exhibition train unloading. There was then a railway running through the city where the Queensway is today, and the Exhibition came to town on the rails. There were flat bed cars in the train with large-wheeled wagons on them. The elephants were used as labor to pull the wagons down O'Connor Street to the Exhibition grounds. My father, my sister and I used to go and watch this event. We would go when the Ex came to town, and then go and watch the train leave the morning after the Ex had closed down. Some of the carnie workers would sleep on the flat bed cars underneath the wagons, and we would wave at them as they left town for the next show. I was born in 1942, so I would think that this happened in the mid to late 40s."

Standing at the apex of the Bank Street Bridge, looking north, as the hometown traffic starts to gum up the works, I'd be happy to award a high Jane Jacobs walkability rating to this section of Bank, somewhere in the high eighties. Yes, more benches and trees please, but otherwise fine retail therapy, an enjoyable outing. Its fate may be to become a sort of living retail community museum—the Glebe Apothecary has already grasped the concept—but as I said earlier, what would be so wrong with that?

Because it is bound north and south by water—the Rideau canal to the north and a lovely, stately stretch of the Rideau River to the south—coming down off the Bank Street bridge into Old Ottawa South feels like coming onto an island. It's my favourite stretch of the street (I used to live in porch-land on Grove, in a foursquare brick house with a great sidewalk tree and a kindly Italian landlord) and besides, after Billings Bridge it all turns into Anywhereville. I haunt the place at least once a month to imbibe a little fair trade tea and to fondly scrutinize antiques I can't afford.

The walk down to the river begins with a classy limestone church, Southminster United, dedicated in 1932 with a hint of Art Deco in it and a terrific organ. It is indeed the uniting of two previous churches, a Methodist and a Presbyterian, one on the same site and one on Sunnyside. Then across the street, in matching stone, the Sunnyside Branch of the Ottawa Public Library, a secular church that handed out its first library cards in 1951, the year *Catcher in the Rye* was published, and listed the modern miracle of air conditioning among its charms. The original Ottawa South Branch was in a vacant shop further south and had been there since 1917. Next door to the new branch is Roy Barber's auto palace, where the very sociable Roy himself set up shop in 1967 and continued doing fill-ups almost until the day he died. When I popped in to say hello, I was treated to a visit to the washroom in order to view the photo collection of the five gas stations that once adorned this section of Bank, back when running out of gas in Ottawa was almost impossible to do.

I have no idea how many hours I've spent in the Mayfair movie palace, seated three rows from the big light, or in the neighbourhood pub next door for that matter, now called Quinn's but at one time bearing the then topical name The Mad Cow. I was booked to sing there one weekend in the Eighties when a few days prior to my gig a stolen car plowed into the place with an under-age driver behind the wheel. I was upstaged by that, for sure. The projectors in the Mayfair are the originals, would you believe, dating from 1932 when it opened and lately they've taken to having music concerts there, for which it is perfectly suited.

At the busy and accident prone intersection of Bank and Sunnyside, on the northeast side, is the only chip wagon in the city I know of that stays open till 4 a.m., its perfume wafting over the insomniac students that live in abundance around here. Akel, the owner and chief fryer, has been there seventeen years, part of the Lebanese retail tradition on this part of Bank, and proudly talks of his two sons the lawyer and the pharmacist.

Sunnyside is the southern edge of the mini-steppe that holds the Glebe, and now Bank Street slopes down with a gentle gratifying curve towards what was once swampland. On the right you'll see a wall mural, which if you are a music folkie, will make sense to you and then if you look down as well as horizontally, you'll quickly realize you are on the Canadian Folkwalk of Fame, an idea made real by among others the good folks at the Folklore Centre. (That's a lot of folking in one sentence.) In no time you are stepping on the bronze maple leaf plaque honouring Bruce Cockburn or the latest addition, the impresario and folk music archivist Sam Gesser. I'll leave it to you to find the mural dedicated to Quebec fiddler Jean Carignan.

You don't have to wait long when strolling the street here to see, usually in rapid succession, people in a state of learning, whether it's on the bagged instrument they are holding on their way to a music lesson, or in and out of Hopewell school, which building by the way is celebrating its centenary in 2010, or boisterously displaying their membership of Carleton University behind a coffee and a laptop or a pint. The laundromat here is as much a social centre as a business.

Architecturally, the new and the old, the bland and the characterful, mix as I drop down the hill, and there's a new apartment infill at Ossington on the west side that holds its own; not as good as the new one on Dalhousie which should win awards, but close. The Old South has an active pride in its heritage and when some crass mercenary notion or other rides into the village and attempts to mess with it, a wily community association that is centred on an old fire hall comes out fighting with the bells ringing.

I cannot remember if I ever attended the Strand Theatre further down, which only showed movies for a while in the early 1950s and then went the way of all bingo. It has been replaced by that cookie-cutter coffee franchise the CBC cannot stop mentioning and holding up as a Canadian icon.

Trinity Church at number 1230 is, well, there is no other word for it, cute, with a day care playground out front, but it too was almost desecrated a few years back in one of those progress—so-called—versus heritage arguments that bubble up like methane every now and then in older neighbourhoods that are prepared to fight back at the developers. It's still there.

And then you can smell the river before you get to it and walk down to the riverbank, where the summer swans hang out and the day trippers used to let the carthorses walk in and take a drink. I know I'm on old, founding homestead land as I stand here, where the lots on the hand drawn maps carried names like Billings and Williams that pre-date the arrival of Colonel By. Then Bank Street disappears under the wheels of cars out into the new south, and I call it a day and sit and watch the river flow.

Beechwood Avenue

The old gates of Beechwood Cemetery.

tanding on the end of the St. Patrick's Street Bridge, with the mercury way down and the cars putting out little clouds of exhaust as they wait for the traffic lights to release them, Beechwood Avenue winds out ahead of me. No doubt there was indeed a fine forest of beech trees here once, brought low to service the mills of the very successful capitalist Thomas McKay and to clear a road to allow the horse-drawn hearses to make their way to the wooded lots of Beechwood Cemetery. The cemetery grounds opened up in 1873 to admit the mostly Protestant dead of higher Ottawa society, who were dying to get in there.

It's easy to figure out as you walk Beechwood that it exists, as it pretty well always has, as a real estate boundary. On your left the streets arrow first into New Edinburgh, then they rise into Rockcliffe's heights. On your right are the level streets of Vanier, although in its infancy this was Clarkstown, named after a Mister T. M. Clark who—smart move—married one of Thomas McKay's daughters. Clarkstown never really enjoyed a growth spurt, having only 150 or so inhabitants in 1891, all but ten of them transplants from Quebec City, and in 1909 it was hitched to the neighbouring anglophone Janeville to create Eastview. New Edinburgh and Rockcliffe are testimonials to the developer's instincts of McKay, who laid them out in the anticipation of attracting the better money that he sensed would begin to populate the town he helped found.

As nuggets of beech wood are used in the brewing process of some malt beers, it is appropriate that the first building on the north side of Beechwood is a live music pub where I've had the pleasure of singing with musical friends on more than one occasion. Moviephiles of middle age and beyond will recall this as the site of the independent, movies-with-subtitles Towne Cinema, in which I indulged my movie addiction till it closed in 1988 and shifted over a short walk to Rideau Street. In summer, the pub's open-air, second-storey balcony is very lively, which contrasts nicely with the cemetery calm at the other end.

Walking the commercial strip of Beechwood there is much to occupy the senses: a little bakery, someone making clothing alterations in a window, a model train set on the sill of the friendly neighbourhood barber, a very browsable independent bookstore and a café specializing in scones, and it is in here that I bump into, if she will excuse the designation, living local history. Heather Matthews, who owns the Scone Witch, is a descendant of both Donald Grant, who was Thomas McKay's secretary, and the Clements family, who arrived here in the mid-1820's with Colonel By. Now that's old Ottawa indeed. A little further on I enjoy the counterpoint of a yoga establishment on the Rockcliffe side of the street offering *Yoga For Real People* (and where do the unreal people go to bend?) and a derelict house on the Vanier side awaiting demolition to make way for a mini-mall.

Although there isn't a single building with a full heritage designation on the street, the pleasantly ramshackle house that now constitutes the El Meson restaurant on the south side comes close. It has won a renovation award, and no doubt in its familial days was not the only one on the avenue with a decent verandah. On the side of the restaurant there is a mural depicting diners, and I realize I am back in mural country. And just after the restaurant is the imposing, sideways on église of the Paroisse Saint-Charles Borromée, whose front lawn is a useful short-cut for shoppers returning to Vanier. The church's spire is still the tallest thing around, and its address is actually on rue Barrette, a name that will be familiar to older francophone parishioners. François-Xavier Barrette, a larger-than-life man in many ways, was the priest here from 1912 all the way up to 1961, and he was a lifelong (he died in 1962) champion of French-Canadian culture, going so far as to institute the 39th company of Canadian Papal Zouaves in 1955, the Zouaves being the Papal guards. The Eastview chapter of the Zouaves, although they were never called on to defend the Pope's person, did march behind their founder on many a feast day. The avenue is less colourful with their passing.

Sensing that the chill in the air has reached my bones, I turn back at the cross-street of Marie to make my way to the neighbourhood brew pub to enjoy a swift half of the dark beer they call Bytown, which seems appropriate to the day. The vista back down Beechwood is capped in the distance by an uninterrupted, quite stunning view of the Parliament Buildings, and for a second I can see the Eastview streetcar coming towards me, followed by a funeral procession on its way to the cemetery.

The half is indeed swift and I move on. The upscale, fair-sized Bridgehead coffee shop on Beechwood, banal, generic coffee-related photos on the wall where there should be local art, is packed on a mid-week afternoon. Yes, there are one or two stroller mums and a designated stroller granny, but there are several couples in chatty amour, and even more soloists firmly encased in the electronic bubble, headphones and a laptop seizing their full attention. World War III begins outside and no one notices.

The road to Beechwood Cemetery has been well travelled by the dead and the mourning for over a hundred and thirty years. The street signs as I get nearer are still the old-school metal black and white ones and they possess a charm the modern green ones, which look more like jar labels, lack. One sign bears the coat of arms of Rockcliffe village, complete with a woodpecker and a heron and a little Latin, *Inter Arboribus Floremus*, which if I dive into the sediment of my education means "We flourish here among the trees." That about sums up Ottawa. Now the houses start to outnumber the stores, and they also begin to sprout front gardens and get considerably bigger, literally in a different class altogether.

The last retail row on Beechwood, before it tree-shifts into Hemlock past the cemetery gates, includes an animal hospital, and in the space of five minutes a fru-fru poodle and a boxer make their way inside. Most of the wooden hydro poles carry adverts for upgrading your body image; there's a booty camp that will help you lose sixteen, not fifteen, pounds from where you most want to. I can't imagine the price of an undeveloped quarter-acre of land in this area—'Just a short walk from the cemetery!'—but, the garage nearby is offering one-hundred-and-twenty-dollar car washes. There is a whack of embassies around here. Just outside the garage are not one, but two Virtu-Cars.

Calling in at the No. 57 fire station, I chat with Frank, Steve and Mike, who are in the midst of a twenty-four-hour shift; the new hours system which got started on January 1st. When the station went up in October, 1987, it was No. 6, and there is some discussion as to when, post-amalgamation, the number got changed outside. The work order took a while to worm its way through the new city hall. When asked, they reply that yes, they have been out today, that morning, to a false alarm on Rideau Street. Unfortunately, while they were responding to that, a real fire was underway on Sheffield Road, a two-alarm blaze in a trailer, and they missed the request for them to attend. Behind them, in the immaculate kitchen, there hangs a row of huge woks, and they too are ready for the heat.

The ramp up to Beechwood Cemetery reminds me of another such rising road, and I was half way up before I recalled it; the incline at the entrance of the National Gallery, a building which from the outside has a mausoleum air to it. Cemeteries are, when all is said and done, sculpture gardens of a particular kind. And Beechwood, as the granite plinth at the entrance says down at the entrance, holds the title of "The National Cemetery."

The first thing available to read on the way into Beechwood is a snow-capped plaque with a poem on it by Archibald Lampman. Lampman came to Ottawa in 1883, and led a quiet life as a postal clerk, and wrote many verses about the Ottawa he saw, including the one on the plaque that perfectly describes the mood and meteorology today of this beautifully landscaped park.

'Here the dead sleep—the quiet dead. No sound Disturbs them ever, and no storm dismays.

Winter mid snow caresses the tired ground, And the wind roars about the woodland ways.'

Lampman is buried here, within his own poetry; he died of a weak heart at the low age of thirty-seven, and his grave is marked not by the monumental but by a plain stone. Then not ten feet beyond, at the entrance to the botanical gardens, is a plaque to one of my political heroes, when heroes there were— Tommy Douglas. Walking up to the gazebo wherein several others are commemorated, these words are on the plaque bearing his and his wife's dates. "Courage, my friends, it is not too late to make a better world." Words that are light years from the petty scripts of the latest round of Con and Lib attack ads that we are suffering.

Across the road, at the site of an old stone office, rows of shiny unmarked stones await the stone carver's chisel and an electronic signboard informs me of the times of the three interments scheduled for today, one with a Chinese name, one Italian, one Scottish. The National Cemetery indeed. I sit down on a cold bench beneath a beech tree and, planning ahead, start to pick the soundtrack for my funeral. Peter Gabriel's *Solsbury Hill* for sure. Then I notice I'm feeling peckish.

Booth Street

Booth and Duke Streets, 1962, now opposite the Museum of War.

*I*f you spent a couple of days writing down all the streets in Ottawa that are named after someone, then arranged them in chronological order by eponymous date of birth, you would have a kind of personality history of the town; a roll call of those who have reached some measure of civic achievement, usually related to wealth accumulation, in their lifetime. The city's household names.

In his day, John Rudolphus Booth was a big cheese in town, more of a lumber duke than a baron; a very, very successful, autocratic capitalist. He was good with wood, built model mills as a child, and was destined from the moment he arrived in the area to become a street name. (Is anybody called Rudolphus any more?) Booth was known simply as J. R. in his lifetime, and his initials were recycled in the 20th century as a Texan television star of similar instincts.) He wasn't born here—he was from the Eastern Townships—but he died in Ottawa in 1925, a couple of years short of having endured to one hundred. The succession duties on his estate totaled seven million dollars.

When it came to naming a street after him, of course it had to be a major one, and so we have Booth Street, running from just off Dow's Lake to the Chaudière Falls, with a major government institution each end. Like Booth himself, it covers a lot of Ottawa history.

I start walking along Booth's backbone at the southern end, at the end of a little path running up from the Dow's Lake where it meets Carling. It is just coming onto dusk, and the first few blocks of the street are very quiet. By day, it is a different scene, crowded from Carling to the Queensway with arriving and departing civil servants. Almost all of them possess livelihoods (for the time being) in some way connected to the land, to the national geography and geology. The national preoccupation with those two natural sciences, the "what's on" and "what's under" of Canada, is headquartered here.

There is actually open land immediately on the east side; a plain bit of grassland that recently received some small fir trees after a big cleanup operation. J. R. Booth conducted considerable industrial activities around here that later, when the pollution laws had advanced, needed cleansing. It hosts one or two picnic tables, a butt stop on a pole, and not much else. There is a small cairn by the sidewalk that requires a flashlight for me to read it. It dates from 1996, and marks the 50th anniversary of the "Establishment of the Army Survey." The surveying instrument atop the cairn is removed when not needed.

On the west, things begin with a gleaming stainless steel flagpole topped by our flag, the signal that you are in government territory. The Earth Sciences building alongside the flagpole is set nicely back, always a good idea with big buildings. Within, the workers occupy themselves with remote sensing, something Canadians are very good at. On the sidewalk there are, count them, no less than seven newspaper boxes, with papers free or for a price and all the real estate listings you can eat.

The imposing, plain yellow-brick complex, the shape of a gigantic staple, runs from 615 Booth to 555 and stretches almost to the Queensway. It is a place whose interior is familiar to me, having spent much time there in the Earth Sciences library researching a book. At the southern end the ISO banners that brighten the walls proclaim that herein are departments concerned with the Atlas of Canada, geodetics (the business of measuring the earth) hydrographic mapping, cartography and aerial photography. Some of the results of generations of aerial photos of Canada can be purchased here.

The central portion of the complex is set back from the road and here in front of it is the rock garden I had wished for in the adjacent grassy openness, as well as a forest of bike racks. Scattered big chunks of limestone and granite are suitably labeled, plus a concrete waste bin that in the fading light I mistake for another exhibit.

The other arm of the staple has a grand exterior staircase leading to it and it is where you gain entry to the Geological Survey of Canada. Founded by Sir William Logan, Canada's first rock star, originally quartered in Montreal, and then housed on Sussex, then within the Museum of Nature and now on Booth as of 1960, the Survey has a tremendous history of exploration and daring explorers, research and of the public locating and mapping of our natural resources to enable their private exploitation. It is staffed by well-grounded people. The bookstore I used to frequent in 601 Booth, once I had got past the death glare of the Security, is closed now, gone. Soon, so I am told, the Earth Sciences library, wherein I learnt much of this wondrous land, is to be closed to the public. My sources tell me that, under this science-is-a-servant of business, government morale in the Earth Sciences on Booth is "seriously eroded."

On the west side, there is a series of buildings that evoke for me the atmosphere and period of H. G. Wells; I can imagine the Time Traveller from his *The Time Machine*, published in 1895, working by day in these redbrick and stone square affairs. The impressive doorways with their limestone lintels have the building's original purpose carved into them, lots of "M" words. The first building erected here in 1909 was full of laboratories concerned with metallurgy. As the small tarnished plaque says to the side of the door, it is the site of the first Mines Branch building, and that this was originally called Division Street before being Booth-ed. It takes me a moment to realize that, although there were several lights on in the other buildings, this one appears deserted. Closer inspection reveals that it is vacant; the asbestos within and the nasty stuff from decommissioned labs is being cleaned up, but I suspect these buildings have a future date with the bulldozer, though surely they must be heritage buildings.

And then I must pass under the Queensway, and a sorry underpass it is too, as are the majority of underpasses in this city. The concrete is showing its age, and the graffiti from the street artists that regularly attempt to brighten the place have been painted over with dull grey. This contest between The Insidious Grey, as I call it, and Fading Colourful, is played out all over the city; the Insidious Grey is winning. Grey cars running down grey streets running between grey buildings. As a citizen who walks our streets, I crave colour. Colour is an endangered concept in Ottawa.

Emerging safely into the light at the end of the tunnel, I walk towards Gladstone past little houses, plus the bigger one with glass brick and curves that would look fine on the Miami waterfront. I feel as though St. Anthony, who was actually Portuguese and a heck of a preacher, is walking alongside me. His eponymous church and schools occupy several blocks of Booth, and it is entirely fair to say that the church steeple, added in 1960, is the religious, and social, focal point of Little Italy. Originally started over in Lowertown, the church transferred to the heart of its congregation in Little Italy almost a century ago; the basement was dug out by gaslight by the parishioners after having finished their day's work. It's looking very spiffy these days, having been refaced thirty-six years ago but still looking fresh. Like a strong old tree it has emerged stronger each time it was felled by fire or renovation.

Walking past the church and its adjoining buildings I enjoy the open smile on the face of the bust of Father Jerome Ferraro, seated on a pedestal in a small garden. He was the much-loved parish priest here until 1972. Apparently a better cook than he was singer, Father Jerome was blessed with a big wide heart, and this mention of his name will put a smile on many older Italian-Canadian faces.

The Plaza Dante, opened about a year ago, is opposite the church and has a European feel to it; central fountain, fixed tables with the opportunity for board games, and a marble memorial wall where I learn that five Ottawan Italians were interred during the Second World War, in faraway army bases. The bust of a rather fierce looking Dante cites him as the founder of the Italian language. As I am passing out of the Plaza, the marble pedestals that flank the entrances bid me *Ciao* etched on their backs.

Carrying on along the east side, looking into St. Anthony's School, I can see into a corridor, which has EVERYONE IS ETHNIC spelt on the institutional wall. A fine Canadian sentiment. The school opened its multi-ethnic doors in 1905 as the Dante Academy. Next door, past the ample schoolyard, there is a large empty building site that to my eyes would make a fine inner city park, but will no doubt end up as, um, let me guess, condos? Then I notice I am moving into Little Asia, which is braided into Booth as you approach Somerset, and the small, well-maintained gardens become more oriental. One house has a front window filled with bonsai trees.

There is a man seated outside the attractive Somerset West Community Health Centre on the corner of Eccles who has the aura of someone who has just received and is absorbing bad news. He is with his dog, which is offering him solace as I read the plaque for the award of design excellence the building received. There is a needle disposal box nearby that I initially mistake for a newspaper dispenser.

Proceeding to the corner, past a very busy inner city car service centre—a dying commercial species in Ottawa—I puzzle over the content of the bright mural at the intersection with Somerset, then notice that it has been signed thus in the top right-hand corner: MAKINDUHCITYPRETTY. Now there is a sentiment I could get behind. In the spirit of "if you can't beat 'em, fund 'em" there is a program called "Paint It Up!" that receives $50,000 per year from the City of Ottawa. The project, according to the city's website, strives to engage youth and operates with the goal of supporting "graffiti prevention, community safety and the beautification of Ottawa neighbourhoods through youth empowerment and community arts." Young, funded artists beating back the Insidious Grey. Neat.

I double back to Giovanni's Snack Bar for a sandwich, and a quick Italian lesson from the kind man behind the counter who is watching an Italian quiz game on one TV, while a soccer game is underway on another. As I am settling the bill he mentions the tradition of a glass of grappa taken together at meal's end. I decline, which may have been a little rude of me. Next time.

Having walked uphill to reach the intersection with Somerset, I now begin to descend northward along the softer flank of Nanny Goat Hill (the local Dominican religious order is said to have kept goats hereabouts). The wind has swept garbage down the street and it has trapped itself in the gardens of the several century-plus old homes along here, or accumulated at the foot of concrete walls for the one or two homes that have stairs leading up to them. The garbage level is unusual for Ottawa the Clean. Most of it, of course, is plastic and related to fast food or sugar drink guzzling.

But almost as an antidote I notice a lot of exterior renovation going on; a porch, the pointing on a redbrick home, coats of paint. This home maintenance, that springs from pride, has been an ongoing process in this neighbourhood since the Great Fire of 1900 swept southwards from Hull and burnt out these streets and homes; all of the older homes here date from 1901-1902.

The traffic now—it is after three—is incessant, and speed bumps—vehicular hiccups—make it resemble a carnival ride. No one is out on their porches at this time, though there are many of those. The older houses end and there is younger row housing either side, the east side row having car stables below and a balcony above that, a design that makes practical sense, I suppose, but is also the triumph of function over form; they seem more like housing than homes.

At the intersection with Albert, the view opens out, as though stepping out of a forest to reveal a prairie, with an arterial road running across it. LeBreton Flats. The Gatineau Hills are visible in the distance as a rumpled blue outline, and directly before me is cleared, scrubby land, fenced-in plots of wasteland with the wildflowers making the most of it before they disappear beneath development. There is the air of abandoned amusement park at the moment, but down here is where industrial Ottawa was born, flourished, and died, and thousands of workers made their daily bread in the timber and manufacturing and salvage trades.

A large NCC billboard announces I'm entering a redevelopment zone, with an artist's rendering on it of what the future Flats will look like. In the fantasy picture happy people wander over the Flats; the odd car cruises along, and development is scarce and spaced out. This area is, the NCC billboard proclaims, "Our passion, our mission!" My mission for the moment being the other end of Booth Street, I take a stone bridge over the narrow canal that ferries water into the nearby 1875 pumping station. The water is low in the canal. exposing a large pipe and two roadside METRO newspaper boxes that have been tossed in, casualties of some passion for vandalism. At the ugly red and concrete rapid transport bus stops, people are statically smart phoning or pacing. Further along there is the sales office of the developer who will be bringing into being the next round of condos on the Flats, the next stage of the "NEW URBAN VILLAGE!" as the company's oxymoronic spin doctors put it. Looking over at the first phase, anything less like a village is hard to imagine.

As I cross the four-lane, east-west commuter highway that cruelly bisects the Flats, and approach the low lying, mostly deserted concrete and copper War Museum, I notice a small gathering outside the doorway. Getting nearer, I can see the lips moving of a suited man standing on a dais. It's a politician, and he is discussing with reporters the cleaning up of the industrial sins of our fore fathers on LeBreton Flats and across the country.

Moving quickly away from this real-time spin-doctor, I pass the great leaning window of the War Museum, and peak into the hall stuffed with war paraphernalia, most of it motorized. Two kids and a mum are cruising the room, the mum reading a pamphlet, the kids swinging on something. Walking past the copper prow of the museum that points at the Peace Tower to the east on Parliament Hill, which I can still see in the distance, there is a de-winged jet and a tank parked outside at the back of the building. The recycling truck is going to have trouble fitting them in come garbage day.

Now I am passing a lagoon of still water, then a square building with the whirring of generators coming from within, more water, another plain building and then looking west, the tamed Chaudière Falls, tied down like Gulliver to harness their kinetic energy. Just months earlier a vacant industrial building on the east side was disappeared by order of the Domtar company; another piece of Ottawa industrial heritage gone, another building flattened rather than repurposed.

The entrance to the eerily silent Domtar compound, not a worker in sight, bears the address 6 Booth Street. I figure that the centre of the pale green steel truss bridge which comes just after it must be the boundary between Ontario and Quebec, and marks where the Street becomes a Rue, and Booth turns into Eddy. There is no sign indicating this, but the bridge's history is on a plaque in English at one end and in French at the other. The first bridge, built here in 1829, to hop scotch over these islands

was timber, and there have been three since. The present one
dates from 1919.

With time on my hands, I spend the next hour roaming the
abandoned and occupied buildings of Victoria and Chaudière
Islands, the eyes in the back of my head on the lookout for security
guards. I am a kid again, hoping over fences and scurrying along
wall tops like a ship rat on a rope, with the still waters of an old
timber slide or a water race constantly on my left or right, finding
graffiti in the most unusual places and sensing the napping bats
in the pitch-black, otherwise vacant rooms. One day this too will
all have changed, perhaps becoming a First People's park, or a
waterfall park, or a theatre district. Or is that too much to ask.

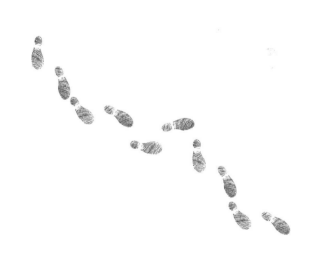

Bronson Avenue

Bronson's mansion, overlooking LeBreton Flats. Destroyed by fire, 1900.

*W*hen a new building in Ottawa raises its lovely, banal or ugly head a temporary barricade goes up around the construction site. Sometimes there are portholes cut in the barricade at eye height, for the viewing pleasure of pedestrians and, no doubt like you, I have spent many an hour over the last few years gazing at the complex, busy-ness of building sites, trying to remember just exactly what was so recently there before it was demolished.

And that is how I begin a walk southwards down Bronson last week, staring over the barricade at the building site dubbed Cathedral Hill. A developer is in the midst of squeezing residencies into the space between Christ Church Cathedral and the fine yellow brick mansion of the Ottawa Diocese offices, and a place of quiet contemplation Cathedral Hill is not. The old church hall has passed under, where once I took part in the pre-death memorial service for Joan Finnigan, the Ottawa Valley's writer laureate. When I look into the hallway of the Diocese office I see a rack of a newspaper called the Anglican Journal. The headline reads "More Budget Woes." There you go.

In an attempt to clear rattling head and ears I cross Bronson and walk over to the railings at the back of the plain small field of grass next to the Julianna apartments at number 100. The view from these railings is mostly terrific, blotted only by an eyesore condo development. A few benches by the railings would be an act of civic kindness.

This conjoined site of the field and the apartments was where Mr. Bronson himself had his mansion, and it stood here until 1900, when it was destroyed by fire. Henry Fielding Bronson had died a very rich man, with three hundred lumber workers calling him sir, the year before. He was a founding member of the "American Club" as I call it, the gaggle of Americans who were essentially given a cheap pass between 1852 and 1854 to come up here and exploit in a lumbering sort of way the power of the Chaudière Falls. Bronson, a Protestant, got stuck into civic enhancement with the founding of a ladies' college and an orphans' home.

Turning to head back down to the bottom of the saddle that Bronson runs across as it heads south, I notice that the developer of Cathedral Hill is advertising it with a banner that states in ad-speak that this is Ottawa's Newest Landmark. I have to say this is demeaning to the word landmark, which should be reserved for buildings with more noble aspirations. The other side of the street on the east side is the condo complex called The Gardens, of which it has almost none. This was the site of another Bronson home, that of Erskine, Henry's son. Erskine decamped to Rockcliffe, and it became a home for the aged, a not uncommon fate for big houses back then. The condos, which are better in design than most, went in in the 1990s.

Rising up from the traffic lights at the corner of Queen, where there is a slalom course of intersecting roads, I pass the side of the shabbily splendid 504 Albert, once the home of a railway executive, now a rooming house. This little area was once known as Ashburnham Hill, and was a swanky address back then in the late 19th century.

Across Slater, on the same side, there is a wasted (in both senses of the word) field, associated with Ottawa Tech, where a brisk pick-up game of basketball played with rusty hoops is in progress in the chilly air. One step above that is a clearly well used community garden, the space packed with raised beds and wilting nourishment. I pause for a moment in this oasis, this ground level space. Nearby a woman in a thick coat is bent over one bed loading what might be potatoes into a shopping bag. What a fine painting she would make, the ugly concrete ramparts of the city over her shoulder.

Backtracking a little and coming up the hill on the west side, there is an intriguing red-brick six-unit apartment block that appears built into the wall of the cut through Ashburnham Hill and is an extension of it. In one window there are paperbacks lying on their side in a shelf unit that faces outward, making it inaccessible to the occupant; it is for the benefit of passers-by, so I check the book titles. Steinbeck, Hesse, all of them classic literature.

That apartment block bleeds into the wall of one of the grandest old homes still standing outside of Rockcliffe and one of my favourites; it is side-on to Bronson, the front door is on Laurier, and it is happy to remain incognito, no plaque. Just about every architectural gimcrack from the Second Empire period is incorporated in it, and it is a feast for the eyes. I have no trouble imagining it being used as the set for *Woman in Black*. I'm told Glenn Gould once gave a house concert here. Then my reverie is broken by the distant sound of serious road construction further along Bronson, and I'm back in the noisy Now.

I have become embroiled lately—the effect of staring hard, while moving at walking pace past the city's architecture— in the design theories of architect Christopher Alexander. He makes a strong case for the elements of beauty in buildings being definable, and he mentions embellishment, imperfection and such micro-details as wooden doors in his writings. I find myself in much agreement with him, particularly on wooden doors. It would be my first bylaw if ever I were to leave my sniper's position and enter the big office. Wooden doors mandatory within city limits.

Only a few paces southward and there are two buildings with just such doors, both bearing plaques, when the Cheney and Davidson families lived side by side and bade each other good morning as they stepped into a car-less street. The Davidson House at 190 Bronson (built in 1889, possibly as a present for his wife) is the headquarters, quite rightly, of the Heritage Canada foundation, while the Cheney House at 176 is earlier, dating from the 1870s.

A gaggle of plainly dressed folks are gathered outside the Bronson Centre in communal smokage, the Centre being a building devoted to providing accommodation for non-profits and a wealth of caring. It is what I call a Good Building, stolidly built in faced stone in 1928 as Immaculata Girl's School for the daughters of parents of modest income. It switched to the compassion business in 1996. And Lady Gaga played the 900-seat auditorium there in 2009. Claim to fame.

Beyond Somerset down to Gladstone is all road works; men in fluorescent vests, machines with piles of old road dirt in their jaws, the laying of interlocking brick to form a wide corner plaza, where doubtless benches will appear, the beep-beep of vehicles backing up. (A friend had a Dachshund dog trained to scuttle backwards whenever he made that backing-up noise.) On several of the hydro poles there are signs declaring DANGER and then DUE TO underneath, and then nothing underneath that. Fill in the blank. I want to write in THE PRESENT GOVERNMENT, but can't reach.

Finding the eccentricities, the eye-chocolate, in this block is rendered harder by the construction circus, but they turn up. The ironwork spiral staircase leading up through the floor to a second floor balcony; the lovely terra cotta carved decal over the vanished side entrance of a fine home; the Doric column that has clearly been imported from elsewhere at the entrance to a small neighbourhood bistro. And perhaps most ironic of all, several of the buildings in this strip have signs on their walls admitting that they are under the care of a property management company called SleepWell.

The game of lawn bowling is hundreds of years old, but I suspect it is struggling to hold on at Central Lawn Green Bowling on the east side, at last I heard down to a handful of members. The leaves on the grass and the shut clubhouse enhance the out-of-season and perhaps out-of-time look, but if there is life in the club yet, I'd love to hear of it.

Then the street character changes as it runs down to the Queensway, starting with the elegant one-storey building on the east side that holds both a memorial architect that's been there since 1925 (hence the fine little Art Deco carving over the doorway) and the more recent, very worthy bicycle recycle "salvation" centre. The street renovations are in an advanced stage here, with freshly laid sidewalk that looks as if it has been extruded like toothpaste from a gigantic tube. The run of buildings on the east side seems to have remained untouched since the 1950s; I can't see them holding out much longer against the condo tsunami, if in fact they don't already have a tick beside them on the developers' hit list. A market storeroom, cardboard boxes piled against the interior windows, then an auto body shop with what must be its original sign, and a dry cleaners with a sign in the window that says, with no tongue in cheek, that they have been Modern dry cleaners since 1948.

Turning back and walking the west side, I pass two cheque cashing and pay day loan establishments almost in succession after re-crossing Gladstone, and I pause to help a mother with a free-range toddler and a stroller up the awkward stairs into one of them. Maybe, fingers crossed, the street facelift will raise the spirit of the street somewhat. Now I'm walking under the Queensway, and no matter which way I face, a chilling wind puts my cheeks in a coma.

The rumble of vehicles on the Queensway and on Bronson overrides the chatter of a lone cluster of Carleton students, their coats bravely unbuttoned, heading for a pint. On a breeze from the past comes the smell of baking bread, from the days when a commercial bakery operated here and infiltrated the car windows as you drove past.

On the east side the old Board of Education building stands almost empty, the concrete stairs cracked, exterior paint fading, one light on inside in a room labeled Furniture. The commercial car garage next door looks suspiciously to me like the work of the architect William Noffke, who built some two hundred buildings in Ottawa and nearby. The date on the garage, which has a red tile roof and white walls is 1930, and Noffke was certainly active at that time in and around the Glebe.

Opposite that, the bright sign of a violinmaker and player lights the sidewalk. The owner, after a life on the road, finally settled here and was inducted into the North American fiddler's hall of fame in 2005. Just up from his store is a large plain building—which if memory serves was once the HQ of the Red Cross Blood Clinic, which opened back in 1959, and before that was an outpost of the Clarke Dairy, whose milk bottles and labels are now collectors items. A sign of the times outside the building tells me that over two hundred realtors are at work in there.

The fast food joint standing next to some empty ground is the busiest thing around as I head south, a pile of cut wood on the sidewalk outside a pizza parlour tempting me to start a street fire and warm up. The streets running off to the east side are treed, wide and flanked by big Glebe houses set back from the road.

Bronson between the Queensway and the Bronson Bridge is a real estate divide: weller-to-dos on the east, houses right on the sidewalk to the west.

I stand for a moment and gaze into the darkened window of a restaurant that makes the modern point of being gluten-free. In the '80s I happily and instructively misspent ten-thousand hours here learning to become a performing musician. This was once Rasputin's folk club, now passed into legend and lies. If the walls of this little space could sing they would produce a choir of the voices of many singers whose names crop up on the CBC with regularity.

At the Northeast corner of the ever-busy intersection at Carling, the other side from the playing field of Glebe Collegiate, is a classic piece of utilitarian architecture, and one of which I'm fond; a brick Hydro substation from the 1930s, a hint of Art Deco in the lines and embellishment of it. (The finest example in the city, Lemieux Island main station aside, is the number 3 substation on the edge of the grounds of the Royal Ottawa Hospital. If these buildings are ever decommissioned and offered as fix-er-up homes, I'm there.)

From Carling down to the Bronson Street Bridge is solidly residential, a few small commercial enterprises on the west side quickly yielding to some David Younghusband-style homes interrupted by a looming condo block which has the decency to be set back in the middle and sport a loggy piece of art in its forecourt. The houses get less solid looking just before the bridge, and then the view opens out at the crest.

And there, off to the side of the bridge, is a bike chained to a lamppost, a bike painted white. It's the ghost bike dedicated to the Carleton University student recently killed in a collision with a car. The wind suddenly blows a little colder, coming off the somber water of the canal, and the sad scene seems to amplify how greatly Bronson's lanes and the adjoining neighbourhood is at the service of the car. People streaming towards their own neighbourhoods have sucked the street life out of this one.

At the intersection of Sunnyside (a good name for a band) and Bronson, the ever-expanding, business-minded university lights up the twilight with the shine from thousands of laptops and cell phones, contrasting with the darker expanse of Brewer Park. Brewer is an urban park with a country feel to it, wetlands and an interesting island-pocked stretch of the Rideau on the southern border, and a fine children's playground on the Ottawa South edge; children who may well grow up to cross the street, attend the university and head out down Bronson out to the airport and into the wide world.

Carling Avenue

The Experimental Farm. Carling Avenue top right.

*C*arling Avenue is almost twenty kilometres long, which makes it a daunting prospect to walk and digest, and so I decide to explore it in miles instead, since it is then only just over twelve. The plan is to start at the Bronson end, which is where I am now and, like the settlers of old, head west until reaching March Road at some point in the future.

Carling Avenue does indeed now begin at Bronson, but in years past it extended to O'Connor. A gentleman prominent in Ottawa history with the splendid, alliterative name of William Washington Wylie, a builder of streetcars, moved upon retirement into 190 Carling, which is now on Glebe Avenue. The seizing of that stretch of Carling by the Glebeites, for which Charlotte Whitton, herself a Glebeite, made a big push, came in the early-'70s.

Appropriately, the modern avenue begins with an automobile repair centre, since Carling is, and certainly was even more so before the Queensway went in, a major east-west artery. The first nine miles run dead straight and are often divided, to the commuters' joy, into four lanes with a central island where pedestrians can pause and gather their courage for the next crossing.

In a few steps I'm past the garage and descending a gentle slope. The south side begins with a bedding store with a punning name and then there is a plain shoebox apartment building with its name, Livingston, beautifully portrayed over the entrance in stained glass. A man in a mask is busy removing graffiti from the front walls with something equally nasty in an aerosol can.

At Cambridge there is a real estate jump and the houses go all mock-Surrey (England) faced with stone on the ground floor and stucco above, substantial porches and miniature country gardens out front, with the phlox in full glory. This is the edge of that hilly enclave sandwiched between Bronson and Commissioner's Park, the one where the tulips mass and whose heads now appear to have all been nipped off by deer, or naughty tourists. The end of one street within the enclave, Jackson, is blocked off at Carling, but just the other side of a row of cedars at the block there is a small, Japanese-ish memorial garden to someone who died in 2012. A good idea for a cul-de-sac that could happily migrate to other parts of town.

The northern side opposite me seems to alternate condos and car parks for Natural Resources workers all the way to Preston, so I remain south side and step onto the grass of the park when it begins, with my left nostril now adorned with the scent of trees in active bloom and cut grass, and my right nostril full of car fumes. Through the trees I glimpse that three-times-life-size statue of the man with one head and a cowboy hat in each upraised hand, and behind him the whiteness of the utilitarian Dow's Lake pavilion.

At Preston I cross over to peer into the induction centre for the ginormous condo tower that will presently begin to lift off on the north-east corner. The sales centre alone is so luxuriously appointed that I wonder if they wouldn't mind donating it as a home for a less-well off family when construction commences. The mind boggles to think of morning commuter exodus out of this colossus. And the "Little Italy" gateway across Preston will most likely live out its daytimes in constant shadow. Looking down Preston now I can see all the way to the Gatineau Hills.

Scurrying back over to the Dow's-Lake side I ascend a grassy knoll that was once the site of a brace of temporary government buildings, erected during the Second World War, that lived on for several decades afterwards. The knoll runs to the bridge spanning the narrow canyon holding the O Train tracks, which have been patiently waiting to link up with sister tracks for many a year now. The station on the north side has an uninviting, post-apocalyptic look. Here's hoping a local designer with flair gets to design the stations yet to come, the downtown ones. On the north side is one of the better- designed office complexes in town, Dow's Lake Court. An effort has been made, dark brown polished stone cladding, dark windows and terraced at the top, so that it doesn't attack your sensibilities as you drive or stroll past it.

Now the avenue begins to rise and I make my way towards the crest beyond which I cannot see. On the grass beside me I pass not one but two soggy abandoned newspapers both of which are opened at the page with a headline wondering if the Senators' captain will return or retire. A nickel says he's good for one more. There is a set of ugly steps elevating me off the street and up into a corner of the Experimental Farm, so I take them, and the world quiets down. In the small outbuildings agriculturalists are staring into computers, and then before me is the now defunct Dominion Observatory building, one of my favourites in Ottawa, designed by architect David Ewart and in operation from 1905 till 1970. The national time signal used to emanate from this building.

Although there were a few houses on the track road, then called Merivale, leading west out of Ottawa before the Farm went in, it was the announcement in Parliament in April 1885 by brewer John Carling, the then fairly new head of the Department of Agriculture, that there would be instituted a model farm for research and knowledge dissemination on the edge of the capital. And so it came to pass, and I am grateful many times a year as I drive or walk through the Farm for the relief from the relentless pace of Ottawa infill. Regaining Carling Avenue, which did indeed take the name of brewer John, I am at the crest of the hill.

The straight rows of the adolescent plants in the Experimental Farm's cropping fields head off southward as I come level with the helicopter-landing pad for the Ottawa Civic Hospital. I cross directly over Carling, pausing for a siren-ing ambulance, and keep walking in a beeline, which takes me up the stone, un-wheelchairable steps of the original elegant entrance. At the top I hop a low railing and stand in the shelter of the wooden doorway. The year 1922 is etched in stone above my head. A grand weathered plaque to the side of the doors informs me that, "William George Black (1846–1922) left the residue of his estate for the maintenance of the grounds surrounding this hospital so that those suffering from illness and from ministering to them might enjoy the pleasure of being surrounded by flowers." Looking up now, there are no flowers in sight, just lots of cars and a delivery van unloading boxes of a pernicious sugar drink. The only night of my life that I spent in hospital was here, and I was here as a visitor many times in the late Fifties when my father was receiving brutal radiation treatment for back cancer.

The mayor in many ways responsible for this hospital was also mayor at the time of the flu epidemic of 1918, which overwhelmed ten thousand Ottawans and killed 652. His name was Harold Fisher; he was a campaigning teetotaler, and a committed Christian and a man very much concerned with the health of the city. After his enlightened leadership in the civic battle to contain the flu, Fisher became determined to give Ottawa a second hospital, away from the potentially contagious mass of humanity downtown. He took a lot of flak for putting it so far out—it was dubbed "Fisher's Folly."

Setting off again I walk past Fisher's statue, which depicts him with his head bowed in thought and his right arm behind his back, with the hospital plans in his hand. Inscribed on the face of his plinth are the words, "If you want to see his monument, look around you."

The next mile's walking takes me through a corridor of buildings, from converted homes, one with a sign on the lawn saying "In Pain?" and giving me a number to call, to ugly, uninspired buildings (the anglophile seniors' residence excepted) concerned with the manifest ways in which the human body malfunctions. An industry has grown up around alleviating and attempting to fix those malfunctions. One such establishment has the word "Shoppe" in its title, which always makes me wince.

Then I'm alongside the Royal Ottawa, the Royal, or as it was known in its early years (it opened in 1910) the "San," because it passed its first six decades as a TB sanitarium. The shift over to dealing with mental disorders began in 1961, and the last TB ward closed in 1970. Again, as with the Civic campus, there are people smoking in clusters outside the doorways, some in wheelchairs, some pacing relentlessly or nodding as though before the Wailing Wall. Also, as with the Civic, there is a sense among the architectural clumps of the ROH campus of hasty edificial expansion trying to keep pace with the growth of the city and its ills. On its website the Royal claims to "connect" with over 60,000 people and families a year; you could do worse if you wanted to study modern Canadian life than spend a year with a big note pad touring the ROH.

Walking on, I pause in a second doorway to pencil some notes.

This is Ottawa Hydro's Sub-Station number 3, housed in one of those attractive red brick Deco looking buildings that dot the city. Looking into the window in the hope of seeing some Metropolis style equipment, all I see is the backs of some lockers. It is with a rare sense of climactic relief that moments later I retreat into Westgate Mall to dry out, something Ottawans have been doing since 1955. Claiming to be Ottawa's first shopping mall, Westgate is the place in Ottawa where the aural pollution that is muzak made its debut. Exiting the Mall the moment I feel slightly dryer, I pause on the side of the ramp leading up to the Queensway and recall the reader who warned me that this is a life-threatening crossing for anyone less than an athlete. There is one of those fascinating rapid bridge, replace-in-one-night type circuses underway on the opposite side of the intersection, so I do a little Zen contemplation of that before stepping out.

It is while walking this third section of Carling Avenue— from the intersection with Kirkwood at the Queensway underpass down to the turnoff to Britannia Park—that I develop a curious thirst. It is for green space, for foliage and grass beneath my feet. I don't need a lot, just the occasional sip of chlorophyll-scented air and birdsong. The unrelenting greyness of the commercial building blocks occupying long stretches of Carling becomes oppressive for the pedestrian. Agreed, the street is not designed for walkers, or marauding journalists, although I do pass the occasional older person making a determined effort to get out.

But the longing arises for some other architect than man and his wallet to shape the surroundings. Or even for some humble eccentricity, like the bright blue Ottawa Church of God building. Silliness, an essential ingredient of any day, is too much to ask for, but some public art wouldn't go amiss. The more the merrier.

During the trudge along Carling, with Carlingwood and Woodpark districts on my right and Glabar Park and Whitehaven on my left, the name McKellar crops up, as in McKellar Park and McKellar Heights, which relates back to John McKellar, who had a substantial dairy farm stretching back from the river west of present day Woodroffe Avenue. I have in my files the investment brochure from before the Second World War for the sale of lots in McKellar Townsite, which ran north to the river from Carling, when the McKellar family decided to exchange cows for accommodation. "You can spell health, wealth and happiness, three of life's most longed for blessings, with two words. And they are—McKellar Townsite." That is about as purple as it gets in real estate copy writing.

I walk all the way to the rapid transit station at Lincoln Fields, past mini-malls and major malls and a brief spasm of residential past Maitland, before I can quench my green thirst. I have to walk for only a few seconds and I am in what seems to be an orphaned cherry orchard of perhaps fifty trees neatly laid out. There's a healthy scattering of Devil's Paintbrush on the path to the orchard, its orange flower snagging the eye with its brightness, the opposite of grey. A five-minute walk from here, after alighting from a bus, and I would be by the river on a particularly pretty stretch, or alongside Mud Lake.

The Olde Forge is a visual curio for commuters waiting for the traffic to get going again at the maze of traffic lights where Carling and Richmond braid into each other. The little log cabin sits on a triangle of grass with cars on all sides like circling wagons. Between the plaque on the door and a framed history page on the wall inside I learn that this was once the home of George and Jane Winthrop, who built a homestead here next to their blacksmith's shop circa 1830, which is seriously old, back when this area was in Nepean township. Robert Winthrop, their son, was born in this house in 1842 and he died here in 1929, both he and the house having survived the terrible fire of 1870. Later, after renovation, the house saw service as a lively tearoom and then in 1958 the City expropriated the property prior to street widening. Of course, a house this old has its resident friendly ghost, that of Jane Winthrop, and its historical point of interest; the big iron gates for Parliament Hill were supposedly forged here and trundled over there in pieces. And Robert, between 1876 and 1892, kept a business journal that I'd like to track down and ingest.

The lady behind the desk inside the Olde Forge explains that it is now a community resource centre dedicated to keeping seniors in their homes as long as possible, and to that end they have a mighty force of volunteers and staff. "Everyone likes working here," she says, "it's a happy place." A session with a group of seniors is just finishing as I arrive. "See you next week," says one of the staff to a man with a walker. "God willing and In sha Allah," the man replies. Just a few steps across the Olde Forge Car Park there is a community garden, with multiple instructions on posts as to how to compost, and stone sculptures by schoolchildren.

A few more steps and some more fender dodging and I'm at the entrance to Britannia Park. The park, in the years it hosted the Ottawa Folk Festival, was a great place for sunset with a soundtrack, but even at midday it is a breath of fresh (ish) air as I walk down the slope towards the pavilion. Once upon another Ottawa, this was the end of the streetcar line and the covered stop is still here. In its heyday Ottawans used to flock out here at weekends in the thousands for the sand and the swing bands. I lie down on a meadowy slope by the baseball diamonds and listen to a hyperactive, courting robin, with the gentle plunk of tennis balls in the background.

Standing on the crest of the hill at Britannia Park looking west, on a day of surpassing perfection, the sun is enhancing the drab appearance of the many high rises on the south side of Carling. The oh so British name of Britannia was imported by Colonel John LeBreton, he of LeBreton Flats, one of Ottawa's earliest real estate speculators who had an estate in the area. In his choice of name he may have been blowing a raspberry at American Philemon Wright on the other side of the river, who had used Columbia as a name for part of his land holdings.

The store names on the little strip malls that hold the high rises apart speak of cities and countries a long way to the east, and the clusters of people at the bus stops are considerably more ethnically diverse than, say, in New Edinburgh. No doubt there is a difference in average income as well. Prompted by one restaurant's name, my thoughts migrate to the Turkish protesters in Gezi Park in Istanbul, a protest that began when developers wanted to replace the park's trees with condos. And within that thought I hear small echoes of the South March Highlands. The housing becomes more residential and a mere two storey as I come level with Andy Haydon Park and turn in. Andy Haydon, a local, in-and-out politician, part pit bull, part terrier, has a fine legacy in this riverside swath of manicured parkland. A couple just ahead of me on the path is holding hands, him in shorts; her in a hijab and abaya. The seeds of the cottonwood trees are blowing in a warm snowstorm off the river and onto the paths and the street. A circle of baby walkers, like Red River wagons making camp, are stationed near a kids' playground that includes plastic water wheels and slides. There is much shrieking, certainly one of the sounds of summer.

I don't know about you, but for me, Andrew Haydon Park is top of the walk among the city parks. All the annual crop of dead fish has been cleared from the big pond, which reminds me of the ponds on the Mall in Washington, and several of the picnic tables are adorned with summer food. A group of seniors from a local residence are bellied up to one, and though quieter than the kids they are all chatting at once, as if in a beer advert. In the lovely mini-Hollywood Bowl with the moat in front three people are rehearsing a performance piece. Two of them are wearing buffalo horn headdresses and declaiming what sounds like a native legend.

A short hop along the riverfront and I'm in Dick Bell Park sitting on a bench in front of a noisy purple martin sanctuary. Mr. Bell was an MP and cabinet minister for Carleton who was born and died in the same house, a heritage home in the Britannia Bay section of Richmond Road. Only one sailboat in the Nepean Sailing Club, which is within the park, is moving. The colour blue is everywhere on the reefed sails and awnings as I walk out to the small lighthouse and gaze a while on the beauty of this inner-city-stretch of the river.

Back on the road, noticing that it's garbage day in Crystal Beach, I do a little scouting for cast offs, always a rewarding thing to do in the richer neighbourhoods. Sure enough, I snag a couple of lawn chairs that are only in need of a paint job. There are some serious mansions here, all turrets and raised patios and three-car garages and stone facades. Among the monoliths there is a small chalet for sale, a remnant of when this was cottage country. A daydream come true for someone.

Moving on, on the south side of the avenue the glass polygon dome of the Nortel campus, as was, pokes above the trees. It's a bellwether now to the perennial ability of successful businesses to have their reach exceed their grasp. Walking on, the roadsides turn to scrub land, with just the odd farmhouse hanging on and Carling straightening out.

At a roadside fruit stand I pick up a pint of strawberries and walk the rest of the way to the junction of Carling and March Road. A road sign informs me that I'm in a high deer collision area, by which I take it to not mean that the deer are on drugs. Shirley's Bay, a name applied both to a superb ecological reserve on Chartrand and Haycock islands at the end of Rifle Road, and a defence establishment on the north side of Carling, beckons, but the sun is at its zenith and a not unpleasant wooziness is spreading through my head on this, the first day of summer. I pass a sign for a canine sports centre, which conjures up all sorts of cartoons in my light head. And here are the traffic lights at March Road. Journey's end, twelve miles from Bronson Avenue. I turn back to the east and finish off the last of the strawberries.

Carp

Carp Memorial Hall at Carp Road and Donald B. Munro Drive.

*T*he wooden bench on the widened sidewalk, outside Faith's general store, at the crossroads of Carp Road and Donald B. Munro, on a sunny spring day, is probably the best place in Carp to eat your sweet potato fries from Brenda's chip wagon.

To reach Carp, I had gotten off the mind-numbing Queensway at March Road and headed north, where the first morsels of architecture I saw were a set of abandoned farm buildings, followed by a large shoebox office building, also empty. Then the hi-techery HQs got going, the other motorists alongside me resented my observational turtle pace (honks and hand gestures) and there were petrol stations and strip malls everywhere inbetween the office towers. The little stone March House that once seemed to be out in the country is now a spa, but it still marked the beginning of the fields, the berry farms and the isolated houses. The Crazy Horse saloon, where once I made folk music for a country crowd that was not listening with great dedication, was gone.

There is now a City of Ottawa blue sign at the junction of the March Road and Donald B. Munro Drive, erected after the great white shark of Ottawa bit into Huntley township in 2001 and amalgamated the village of Carp. Which, it seems likely, is named after a fish, but not that fish. *Carpes a cochon* is French for sucker fish, and the thin, pretty river that skirts south of the village and floods every year once held suckers a plenty. The river has an official, active set of friends who care about it and work hard to let it be it itself and remediate the effects of modernity. And Donald B. Munro was a farmer who in 1897 moved into where the village is now to take over a brick works and continue farming.

I walk into Carp central down farmer Munro's eponymous road, going along and then down a ridge, past a garden centre no doubt grateful for spring to have sprung, and an establishment offering yoga and tea. The times they are a changing, and yoga and tea are both in the ascendant just now. They have reached Carp. Next comes the beginnings of a small subdivision where they are leveling the ground to plant rows of houses. The heavily ironic title of the sub-division is Green Meadows.

The established homes after that are at ease with themselves, ranging from the smaller ones with porches crammed with geraniums in pots to the grander mini-mansions set back from the side walk, interspersed with a business or two dedicated to self or home improvement and then the noise of the flour mill trumps the passing pick-ups.

Which brings me to the chip wagon, and then on to the bench I opened with. Opposite me at the crossroads is the Community Hall, a plain-enough affair erected in 1921 but nicely landscaped out front. A mother and child emerge from the early-years centre at the side and both greet me with a singsong hello in different keys, while two women conduct what I call an organ recital on the sidewalk, in that they began their chat by swapping tales of their internal organs and how they were faring. Happily it is a short recital.

Staying on flat ground I rise reluctantly from the bench and continue on Munro, nodding hello to the pizza maker on a smoke break and noting that the dry cleaners and car wash are in the same building; a place to make a clean break of it. The river is visible between buildings and across a field. At the bend in the road I contemplate a swift half in the very pleasant Britishy pub just up the hill, resist temptation (there is no such thing as a swift half) and turn around on the bridge over the river. It was near this pub that, in 1844, young James Paul, a shoemaker, set up shop on a mere half acre. Not being a farmer, Paul was the unwitting first resident of Carp village to arrive, although he only lasted a handful of years.

A longer walk takes me down the Carp Road north, past the closed fairgrounds and out to the entrance to the Diefenbunker. In September, I and many others will be in the bleachers for the Carp Fair, which is what a fair should be (Ottawa City please note), octagonal exhibit hall, large horses and fancy chickens, fried food and risky rides providing cheerful nausea and lots of ways to lose money. I've arrived a little too early for the farmers' market, whose sign is still fresh and which is due to start up at the weekend.

As for the Diefenbunker, which is a modern, just-in-case folly dating from the Cold War and is strange enough inside to have appeared briefly in a Ben Affleck action film, I have walked its anachronistic corridors only once on my way to the rooms where the Bytown museum stores many of its overflow artifacts. It was a creepy experience. The town library sits just outside the bunker gates and is much busier. The pen is mightier than the sword.

Back on my bench, my circumnavigation complete, change seems to be in the air in Carp, though not as a strong wind but more of a breeze. Although there was a hiccup in construction, the large rest home in the middle of the village is due to go ahead, and little subdivisions besides Green Meadows will arrive soon enough, to be sure. But, to my mind, there is an air of comfortable take-us-as-we-are about the place, as opposed to say Merrickville, which has put on its party frock and beckoned city folk to visit its tourist trap main street. Hopefully, the wind of change will not blow quite so hard down Carp main street.

Chaudière Bridge

The first Chaudière Bridge, 1828.

*I*t's only when something becomes suddenly unavailable, something like a bridge over the Ottawa River that appreciation for it goes up. The many thousands of commuters and day travellers who took crossing the Chaudière Bridge once or twice a day for granted were snookered by its closure last week, and they immediately wanted it back. They missed it.

The daily view out the car window for those bridge-using commuters, which they also take for granted, with their minds fixed on getting to work, is actually a darn good history lesson. Travelling north to south, from Gatineau to Ottawa, from province to province, from Lower Canada to Upper Canada, from Wrightville to Bytown, there is immediate evidence of the region's huge role in the lumber trade in the paper plant to the left and in the making of power to the right. Continuing on, there is the old Wilson Carbide mill, and to the back is the log-ringed Algonquin settlement, a living reminder of the fact that the islands, according to the 1763 Royal Proclamation, are Algonquin territory till the sun cools, and that that proclamation has never been overturned.

The common historical denominator for all enterprises is the falls, the step down in the limestone river bed that sends water thundering towards the St. Lawrence and from there to the gulf and the ocean. The Algonquin, who had been living around here since before the Christian movement got started, held appeasement ceremonies at the side of the falls. The soldier, seaman and trading-route seeker Samuel de Champlain noted the power of those falls on his way through here in the summer of 1613, and the many entrepreneurs, most of them American and one big Canadian—J. R. Booth—who clustered around the falls and first tamed them, used their power to run their mills. Those mills, relics now for the most part, were once members of the biggest conglomerate of sawmills in the world.

The other thing commuters notice as they pass under the green metal latticework of the central bridge, is that they are hop scotching over a series of islands. It was the fact of this mini-archipelago sitting conveniently in front of the falls that focused the mind of Ottawa's first bridge builder, Colonel John By, the man who also engineered the arduous, deadly construction of the Rideau Canal. In an old surveying sketch dating from 1824, done by a Major Eliot before there was any bridge across the river, you can count seven islands, and laying a ruler along their axis, it becomes obvious that a series of short and longer bridges will connect riverbank to riverbank. The greatest span would be 100 or so metres.

In the fall of 1826, By got orders from his boss, Lord Dalhousie, who later reincarnated as a main street in Ottawa, to build such a series, since much of the timber and nutritional supplies for the canal workers would be coming from Wrightville, the eponymous mill town established by an American from Massachusetts a quarter century earlier, which by then already had a population of several hundred. By first had to clear up a spot of bother at the southern end of proposed bridge line, namely the owners of the land where bridge would meet mainland. He settled it by purchasing the land and reinstating the two gentlemen, Firth and Berry, who had wisely built a pit stop there for lumberman awaiting their log flumes funnelling past the falls.

By, with the assistance of Thomas McKay, duly cast a set of bridges across the gaps between the islands, using stone over the smaller gaps and a slightly arched wooden bridge over the big one. As often happened with first-time construction events in the 19th century, people got killed in the making; a supporting cable snapped and three workmen were tipped into the vigorous waters and could not be rescued. If a contemporary watercolour is anything to go by, the arced wooden bridge itself, when completed, was beautiful in its simplicity and it could carry a load of six tons, not bad for the time. It did however have a best before date, and it collapsed in the spring melt of 1836, after having been shored up two years before. The bridge was closed by official order just two weeks before it collapsed.

There being no other way to get there from here, for several years thereafter two ferries were the only passage across the Ottawa, one for foot passengers from about where Bank Street would meet the river if it were allowed to, and the other for goods from a wharf below Nepean Point. The absence of the bridge was an irritant to the twin growing towns on the opposing river banks, and there was a collective sigh of relief when, in 1842, with winter coming, the Board of Works put up notices inviting tenders for a new bridge.

This second bridge finally opened for carriage traffic in 1843. It was of the suspension variety, designed by one of the Keefer family, a dynasty of sorts that built much that is good and lasting in Ottawa. Since it was seen to unite the two Canadas, it was given the name Union, which is still its official handle, though the colloquial name Chaudière is the common usage. However, it was of a width, twenty feet, that soon became constricting over the years as the number of vehicles using it multiplied, and after decades of use it was due for replacement.

This bridge was indeed replaced in 1889 by the one our great-grandfathers called the "Old Union Bridge," and this time it was built by the outside firm of Rousseau and Mather. There are fashions in bridge building and Rousseau and Mather switched from suspension construction to a steel truss. The large span was again elegant and similar to the suspension bridge that crosses the St. Lawrence in Old Montreal with a tower on each corner, but it had no way of knowing that the Germans were already producing something called the automobile, and that Misters Olds and Ford were going to put the bridge to the test in the years to come.

Within a mere thirty years the back of the Old Union had become too weak for the loads it had to carry, and in 1919 a contract was awarded to the Dominion Bridge Company of Lachine to build the modern bridge that now, in its turn, is demanding some remedial work, after having had half a million dollars spent on it just three years ago. And one wonders if Mr. Murphy, he of the law that states that if a thing can go wrong it will, was in town a little while back, and divined that the bus strike was coming.

The story of Ottawa's bridges spans one hundred and eighty years, and it is still up in the air. The debate over the where and when of the next one is coming to the boil, meanwhile there is a bridge alongside Lemieux Island crying out for decent, non-car usage, and the McDonald-Cartier is an eyesore. Perhaps the Old Union is trying to tell us something about the way forward across the Ottawa.

Dalhousie Street

Dalhousie Street, 1882.

I step into Mello's restaurant on Dalhousie, which opened the doors in 1942 and hasn't closed them since, and refresh my memory of historic photographs of Ottawa that venerable no-nonsense dining location has on its walls. The cashier asks me if I want to eat something or just stare. I explain my purpose and my newspaper affiliation; she says, poetically, "Ah, so you're a streetwalker."

The ramparts of hotels and condos barely visible at the southern end of Dalhousie are veiled in heavy snow as I street-walk towards them from Mello's, giving the view a post-apocalyptic, nuclear winter feel. I'm also moving towards the sleeping quarters of Ottawa University's students, just the other side of those ramparts, with the Salvation Army on George coming up on my left, so the personality of the street shifts from beauty salons and funky emporia to fast-food outlets, clubs, two pharmacies that date from 1920 and 1921, before pharma went big, one art gallery, several decent restaurants and a parasitic place that deals in selling money, cashing cheques and buying gold. In fact I start adding up the number of shawarma restaurants along the southern end of Dalhousie and stop counting after six. A swarm of shawarmas.

As well as being mentioned on the street signs, there are now banners on the faux-old world lampposts that tell me I'm in the serious part of the Byward Market; it's theme-park branding for the benefit of tourists, and it erodes authenticity, but it adds a bit of colour. The symbol on the banner shows a smiling farm boy with a basket of produce between his arms, and a guitar standing up beside him.

Continuing down the dukes—Clarence, York, George—I come to what is probably the best piece of architecture on this strip, the one I call the Mercury Building. It was once the RCMP headquarters, then a francophone department store and then was reinvented, complete with a transplanted statue of Mercury, who is capped with snow at the moment. The architect who did the redesign now resides within, as does the Swedish Embassy; I always wondered where that was. On the opposite corner at Rideau, as there has been a long while, is a convenience store, the Windsor Smoke Shop, and the place where many of us went for, um, head gear, and cheap Halloween masks of Brian Mulroney or some such. The store is what must now be the oldest building on Rideau.

The cut-off-worm-segment portion of Dalhousie on the other side of Rideau continues the fast-fooding, and I slip in to enact some central heating with a little box of poutine. It's a franchise actually, started by a poutine pusher, business-grad type from Toronto. The walls are covered with mounted newspaper clippings, and again here we have advertising in the place of art. It's a spreading branding practice; after we have a moratorium on the impossible to achieve word "closure," can we do likewise for active branding? The veggie version, heart attack in a box, warms me up though. (Poutine was of course invented by a Captain Poutine, who during the siege of Quebec was ordered by his commander to create something out of the slim rations of potatoes, curds, flour and rancid beef stock they had left.)

And then here at the end is a statue of a bronze man staring northwards back down Dalhousie. Obviously it's Lord Dalhousie himself, or a famous Canadian politician but, no, it's Simon Bolivar. The statue was offered to the city in 1988 and then Mayor Jim Durrell accepted it, presumably out of politeness rather than relevance. Out of the corner of his right eye Mr. Bolivar can observe people entering and leaving, in various shades, an "advanced" tanning salon. Advanced?

Getting out of the snowstorm again, I retrace my steps and enter a doorway next to where the big Book Market used to be; I spent many an hour in their lower floor literary section, and once took a bunch of young people from Operation Go Home I was working with there to let them pick a book of their choice. Two of them chose Romeo and Juliet, and then they all asked, quite rightly, if they could have a movie as well.

Two flights up and I enter a large room full of rare and antique books that transferred here from the Glebe about a year ago. The contrast between the bookstore and the street below is vast, and my eye is drawn to a framed poem hung on the end of one of the shelves. It's by John Newlove, and it's signed; a brilliant writer, Newlove lived in Ottawa from 1986 till his death in 2003. The opening lines of the poem that I jot down in my wet notebook, are: *"I'd like to live a slower life. The weather gets into my words And I want them dry."*

Eddy Street

1920's Eddy Street postcard.

The man sitting at the picnic table by the casse-croute finishes his hot dog and lights a cigarette, using a match. He is on Rue Eddy, in Gatineau, a street that for me is among the most walkable in the capital district. It was not far from this casse-croute that, around 160 years ago, young American Ezra Butler Eddy built a shed and he and his wife, Zaida, burnt the candle at both ends making sulphur matches by hand. By the end of his life, in 1906, Ezra was the lord of matches in Canada, also of paper-making; his mills had survived two major fires, crippling debts, and he was a philanthropic multi-millionaire. It was he, as an MLA (he was also mayor of Hull Township) who introduced the bill that created the city of Hull, alias Wrightstown, alias Gatineau.

The man throws his match onto Eddy Street and walks down to the Bistro-Bar L'Original at 104 Eddy which is in full swing, mid-afternoon, and "That's the Way I Like It" blaring out as the door swings open to let out a woman in a motorized wheelchair and lots of bags hanging on the back of it. The bar was originally the general store of Messieurs Deschamps et Carrière, and it is one of several red-brick, dormered buildings on Eddy that are well over a hundred years old.

My stroll up this street of multiple personalities began about an hour ago at the north end. The streetscape is built for walking; olde-style lamp posts with twin hanging baskets, small, too small, trees in boxes, well-used benches on most corners and wide, bricked sidewalks. The giveaway that I am on the Quebec side of the river lies in the working class architecture of the two-storey homes and stores, with their concrete doorsteps, wrought iron balconies, sandwich-board roofs. The artist Henri Masson, who died a mere decade ago in Ottawa, portrayed these streets so well, often in winter with kids at play outdoors. (Kids...Outdoors!) As in his paintings the real life buildings don't seem to have a right angle in them, at least at this end of the street, which has yet to feel the tightening bear hug of gentrification.

The reason it has taken me an hour to walk a mere three blocks is the presence almost opposite each other of a second-hand furniture store and a vegetarian restaurant, both of which I am powerless to pass. The restaurant is replete with lunchtime civil servants who have walked down from the Kafka Komplex at the river end of Eddy, the government ramparts that make the Hull waterfront so hideous. Looking north on Eddy towards the Gatineau Hills the government Casino rises up in the distance, a beacon of high-stakes risk, revenue and ruination. A tunnel connecting the waterfront civil servant buildings to the Casino would keep the money turning nicely in a circle.

When I arrive at the Larouche Pharmacy a block further down, one of those redbrick buildings I mentioned, I pause on the sunny side of the street to take notes. There has been a pharmacy on the premises at 164 Eddy since the beginning of World War I, which is pre-Big Pharma, so your remedy was often mixed up from glass jars right in front of you. The Picards, who took over at the end of the war, held it for eighty years, and one of the second-generation Picards, Giliane, was among the first women pharmacists in the province. She had to get, in the Fifties, her license in Ontario: Quebec didn't consider women capable of professional healing back then. The pharmacy transferred into the healing hands of Roger Larouche in 1988 and remains there now. Not content with revitalizing his neighbours, Roger has been an unflagging force in the ongoing revitalization of Vieux-Hull.

Walking on southwards, from the halfway point on rue Eddy towards the overblown government buildings, I pause outside a high-end haberdashery, an outpost of a Montreal firm. In the middle of the store, which sells shirts at fifty times the price I just paid for one in the nearby, très occupé St-Vincent de Paul, a model is posing for a cameraman.

That a store selling its wares in that kind of price range would think of opening on Eddy is a sign of the new times coming to this end of the street. It is to be hoped that those times do not push out the more eccentric retailers that give the street its walkability. A veteran store a few doors away from the haute mode emporium has baskets of small angels for sale on the sidewalk in front, and its windows are full of spiritual paraphernalia. Long may its wings beat. As has happened on the east side of Sussex, if a street swings too far over to the higher-income consumers, something is lost. Walkability walks away.

Most of the rest of the street is devoted to talking, keyboarding and supping. Several cafés, all of them non-franchise and loaded with personality, are strung along the west side of the street. The notice boards outside these cafés, and their sister cafés and health food restaurants around the city, are snapshots of a counter culture to the McCafes that is thriving and growing.

Another sign of things to come a little further down, on the threshold of the government takeover of south-end Eddy, is the small bright yellow bungalow with benches out front that sells craft beer, craft chocolate and the like. My pleading taste buds pull me in. Allow me here to raise a cheer for the beer revolution of the last decade, the shift to real ale. Opposite this store is a one-storey Heritage Canada building with, ironically, absolutely nothing heritage about it.

Just before the Godzilla office blocks overwhelm the end of the street, there is a small Zen-garden, the size of a large groundsheet. Whether it is temporary or not (the condos next to it on the south-side are new and it may be paired with them) it is like a miniature painting stuck on a grey wall. After a brain-refreshing pause in the park, as I walk towards the famous Bank Hotel, I look back, and see that some clever artist/advertiser has half a dozen bicycles riding up the side of the building housing the cycle store at 136. The new glass and steel government building at 22 Eddy, workplace of 4,000 transplanted civil servants, rises up like a space ship's prow above the hotel.

The Bank Hotel, a true heritage building, looking smart after its new soft green paint job and façade tidying up, stands on land that was originally the property of the Wright family, the city's founders. It sits on the corner with Promenade du Portage, and is now easily the most eye-pleasing building on the street. The doors opened on the Bank in 1908, when Eddy was still called Bridge Street and it was owned by Messieurs Fortin and Gravelle, who started out in lime mining. The local temperance society spent a few years trying to get it shut, and then Prohibition kicked in everywhere but Quebec, and it has been wide open ever since.

Elgin Street

Late 19th-century Elgin, looking north.

The right moment to view the War Memorial on Confusion (Confederation) Square at its most dramatic is at dusk, on a crisp clear November night. They've got the lighting right, and the winged figures atop the crowded arch—representing Peace and Liberty—seem to have just landed out of the darkening clouds. The faint sound of canned Irish music drifting over from D'Arcy McGee's pub does nothing to puncture the ambiance of respect, in fact it enhances it.

The site of the War Memorial (which is officially known as The Response) at the head of Elgin Street has itself changed dramatically, from a dirt cart road over the sturdy Sappers' Bridge in the 1830s to the bifurcated, streetcar-carrying Dufferin Bridge with the canal and railway lines below. These days it's called the Plaza Bridge, which I didn't know till I read the plaque. The gap in the V of the Dufferin Bridge was filled in to support the War Memorial, all 535 granitic and bronze tonnes of it, which was intended as a focus of respect for the First World War dead, but not officially dedicated until 1939, just months before the Second World War got going.

When the triangle that is Confederation Square was done over a few years ago, they opened up a way down to the canal again, a marvellous idea. There's a gallery of life-sized statues ringing the steps down to ground level, fourteen in all, most of them warriors of course, but there is one woman, Laura Secord, and one First Nation representative, Thayendanegea or Joseph Brant as the English called him. Brant was a Mohawk war chief and spokesman, farmer, landowner, linguist, translator, slave-owner and negotiator who came into Canada from the States in 1784, and is actually buried in Brantford. He is worth a movie.

Looking down Elgin Street from the south side of the monument it's clear it has a split personality, all big institutional buildings and monuments at one end and, after you pass Lisgar and the Knox Presbyterian Church, a row of bars and eateries and little stores for this and that as far down as Gladstone. The traffic lights cluster after Lisgar like a festive runway at night; that's the bit a former mayor dubbed Sens Mile.

From the noble austerity of the monument I slip across into the home-goers and lingerers on the west side of Elgin Street and head south, pausing for a moment outside the Langevin Building to beam thoughts of peace and harmony into the Prime Minister's office housed in the Miramachi sandstone Langevin Block. I'm dropping these stony references in because a couple of weeks ago I took what's called a geo-heritage walk in Upper Town under the fine guidance of Mister Quentin Gall. There's a solid book of geo-heritage walks by Gall you can pick up if you want to take your time one afternoon before stealing home or of a weekend, and get truly stoned.

Cheek to cheek with the Langevin Block, limestone to sandstone, is Noffke's 1939 Post Office, built in my favourite architectural period, Art Deco. Though it is listed as being in the Chateau style, the Deco touches are there in the curved corner and the rising exterior clean lines, in the wonderful bronze door panels and the ironwork grills on the windows composed of whale flukes and maple leaves. Oddly, the Post Office clock was two minutes slow of the Peace Tower, which chimed five as I crossed Sparks Street, and approached but did not enter D'Arcy McGee's, where I could see the tops of drinkers' heads through the street level window. I have only performed at D'Arcy's once as a musician; it was exhausting.

Darcy's is the corner of the splendid Scottish Ontario Chambers, built in 1883 for lawyers and the like, a many-windowed, red-brick affair on the upper floors that is everything the nearby Brutalist National Arts Centre, which opened in 1969, is not.

Norman Mailer called that style of architecture totalitarian, and I agree with him; it's a building only an architect could love, and contains absolutely no clues to its function from the outside. Definitely best viewed at night. The Chambers row between Sparks and Queen, however, which also contains Confederation Square's oldest building, the petite, cute 1867 Bell Block in the middle and Central Chambers at the end, built to house railway offices, has a pleasantly old world feel to it. It must never suffer a scavenging attack by condo vultures.

Crossing over I take a seat next to a life-size Oscar Peterson, as the Queen did in June of 2010 when she unveiled the seated statue of him at the southern extremity of the NAC. It's almost kitsch with a half piano coming out of the wall, and him tinkling the cold ivories, but it works. Oscar was rendering "You're Too Marvellous for Words" at the time, to a pair of young French girls. They were unsure of the melody, but by the end he had them humming along.

For a moment, standing in Confederation Park next to the splendid Aboriginal War Veterans Monument, amid the chattering civil servants from Health Canada and nearby offices on lunch/smoke break release, and looking over at the Lord Elgin Hotel, it is possible to suppose I am in London. The hotel, named like the street after James Bruce, first GG of the united Canadas, opened in 1941, at the tail end of Art Deco, and was basically an alternative to the Chateau Laurier for those connected to the war, in town on military business. Small rooms, and, as they say about cheap underwear, no ballroom. The copper roof came at the insistence of Prime Minister King, so it went with the downtown theme. I've never stayed there, but it's an uplifting, soaring building to look at, coming at the end of a phalanx of glass boxes.

I walk on past Fort Court, as I call it, the Ottawa Courthouse, 1986, wondering if the holding cells below are full today and then comes the contrasting elegance of the old 1874 Normal School, now an annex of City Hall. No sign of the mayor looking out of his window; no doubt he's busy attending a gathering of voters somewhere, or more likely chairing a meeting. The "Normal" which I always wondered about, refers to the "norms" of teaching that were passed on there. Unbelievably, the fate of the building was in doubt for two decades, after the teaching of teachers moved out in the early 1970s, when the dead hand of government wanted to put a high-rise of government offices in its place. The heroic Heritage Ottawa saved the day and the walls, and the elegance of the Heritage building now shows up bulky Fort Court; a swan next to a bulldog.

Past Lisgar it's as if Elgin Street changes clothes. The street gets out of its suit with the little Canadian flag lapel badge, and puts on some jeans and a tight sweater. It's a highly walkable stretch of road all the way down to Gladstone, with plenty of shop-window eye candy like that in Perfect Books and Mags and Fags (where *Tattoo* magazine sits next to *Railfan Canada* in the window) and a smorgasbord of nose treats—bakeries and sugary shacks and of course coffee-and-conversation houses. It feels more like the original name the street carried, Biddy's Lane, than a grand boulevard named after a lord.

I should have done this walk on Wednesday, because the Knox church is offering lunchtime organ recitals on that day. A church with the name Knox has bounced around the city, starting way back in Bytown in 1844. The present one went up in 1932, after its very grand predecessor further north on Elgin was knocked to the ground as part of Mackenzie King's big plans for Confederation Square. Because I have never counted them, I hadn't realized there is in fact a trinity of churches on the east side of Elgin. After the Knox comes St. John the Evangelist, which has one of those billboards outside with a moral saying on it; being a bilingual city, there is one saying in English from John Kenneth Galbraith, and one by Abbé Pierre. Pointers for a different kind of good life from the bilious stream of real estate advertising that runs down our streets these days. And on the corner of Lewis sits the quiet Eglise Unie St-Marc, the centre for francophone Protestants in the city. Originally down on LeBreton Flats, the Protestants moved in when the Unitarians moved out in 1965. Same God, different management.

The neon sign reading ELGIN is still on the redbrick building opposite the Knox church, an illuminated echo of the days when it was a cinema instead of a fast-fatty-foods plex. The notion of multi-plexing cinemas with multiple screens all showing something different started here, and it enjoyed a world premiere back in 1948 with the film *Sleep, My Love*, in which the Canadian star Mary Pickford had a secondary role. When the theatre closed, for a brief shiny moment it looked as if it might become the home of the Great Canadian Theatre Company, but that was such a good idea City Council nixed it.

The trick to enjoying Elgin is to check out the second storeys, as well as the storefronts. There is an attempt at 220, for instance, to make the building Deco and, looking over the top of the store at the corner of Cooper, I can see the side of a fine stone house. It turns out there is a heritage designation application in the works for 201 Cooper. It's apartments now, but was obviously a grand house in its turn-of-the-century heyday, and the best guess is on Henry Horsey as the architect, the same man who designed the Nicholas Street jail.

The presence of Minto Park between Gilmour and Lewis makes the street all the more pleasant to perambulate, and if I could institute a Phil Jenkins by-law it would be that there has to be a small park every six blocks in Ottawa, roofed with solar panels in the winter projecting heat downward. Within Minto Park at the back is the monument to women in our town who have fallen victim to violent partners. The women are commemorated in granite crystal-like tombstones, and it's a monument you hope doesn't get any bigger. At the front of the park is a statue, a bust of an Argentinean general and liberator; no offence, but what on earth is it doing there? I presume there is a reciprocal park somewhere in Buenos Aires with a statue of, say, Louis Riel.

Passing Woody's, a pub that for a brief moment actually had regular imported jazz, and gave Ottawa what it so sorely needs, a legendary jazz destination, I notice that the Jack Purcell centre is looking good after a face-lift. Quite a few years ago I just managed to catch the tail end of an Ottawa musical institution there—the Hoots. As I walk back and check out the mushroom project in the garden at the front of Elgin Street Public School, a woman in a bunch of sidewalk strollers says, quite loudly, "I want to shoot the person that did that—in the head." To what she is referring I don't know, but I am two blocks along before my columnist's eye comes back into focus and I find myself outside the Manx, a bar that gets just about everything right in my opinion, including no TV, live music and real beer.

After Gladstone, particularly on the east side, there's a parade of low-rise apartment buildings with names like the Wallace, Park Square, the Royal Court, and the Queen Mary, names that speak of an earlier Ottawa still umbilically connected to Britain.

(On the other side of the street, one of the more sombre, almost shabby Gladstone apartments has a blow-up woman out on a balcony.) Just a bit north of the Gladstone, at number 408, there is a cute little house sandwiched between two taller buildings, and it instantly reminds me of the house the old man lives in, in the animated movie *UP*.

On the corner of Argyle, I turn around. The cop shop is on the opposite side, a truly ugly building that looks more a bunker than a palace of law and order; it was opened by the Prince of Wales, who has publicly declared several times how much he hates that style of architecture. After that Elgin crosses under the Queensway and then peters out.

Waiting to cross over and pass an hour in the Museum of Nature, the man next to me, a gentleman of the street with the wrinkles of hardship about his face, turns to me and says, "Sir, merry Christmas," and I wish him the same. Maybe even more so.

Gladstone Avenue

The Salvation Army Citadel Church 1911, 391 Gladstone.

*T*here are as many paw prints in the snow at the intersection of Parkdale and Gladstone as there are footprints. It's a dog-walking sort of day, only mildly freezing and it's not, right now, *snowing*. As I begin to trek the slushy sidewalk east on Gladstone, heading downtown, a man and his mutt, in matching scarves, pass me.

Ambling down the clean, red-brick south-side wall of the Parkdale United Church Complex, a smartly dressed, be-hatted man is about to enter the side door when he pauses and kindly asks if he can help me. This is the Reverend Bailey, the parish's minister, and in no time at all he has pleasantly explained most of the church's activities and the changing character of the neighbourhood. Included in the former discussion are the pre-school that has run within the church for thirty years, and the one-hundred-and-sixty meals, on average, that will be served through the *In from The Cold* program. Included in the latter, the neighbourhood, he says there is increasing gentrification, which I will soon see for myself as I journey on, and increasing numbers of men not too far away from where we stand that are sleeping under the O-Train bridge. Mind the income gap.

The Reverend, whom I am glad I met, sincerely wishes me a good, warm day and I walk on, past the clubhouse of the Knights of Columbus, where, should I wish to do so, I could partake of a bean feast every other Friday. The side streets on the south side of Gladstone are dammed at their ends by the grey ugly soundproofing walls of the Queensway, which has cleaved through the neighbourhood since the early Sixties. People here and in Otawa East I've talked to who are old enough to recall their communities before they were bisected by the highway talk of it as a scar.

The progression of modest, stand-alone homes, many of them with more than one mailbox to the side of the front door, heads in a straight line due east. The majority of them carry a ground level porch and some have the bonus of a balcony above that, including the duplexes. Connaught Public School, though relatively new, has a timeless look, its brick and stones and curved lintels stating its noble purpose. Looks like I am too late to register for kindergarten. The newer non-brick row homes beside the school are all right angles and are without a porch, without an observation post. This makes them look somehow underdeveloped, stunted, less homely. In the midst of this, as I have seen on other, older middle-income streets, is a mini-mansion with several ice candles on the snow-banks flanking its grand porch. A wealthy merchant's home, once upon a time.

By the time I reach the dogleg in the road at Fairmont I've passed two corner stores, two auto repair outfits and two outdoor telephone booths, which I think makes it a rare stretch of Ottawa roadway. A young woman, puffing on a a cigarette, is actually using the phone booth on the wall of the Fairmont Confectionery, with a bus stop and bench and a small lottery sandwich board surrounding her. The image seems to have come from an earlier epoch. The windows of the confectionery are full of posters and adverts, like a compressed Times Square.

Moving on, and the international-style, heritage-worthy lines of the former Canadian Bank Note building, which began making money as the British North American Bank Note in 1949, catches the eye on the other side, all tidy and unoccupied. The factory was made redundant by the switch to polymer bills. At the crest of the hill at Bayswater I can look downhill towards the busyness of Preston and up the hill on the other side towards St. Anthony's spire, which makes me realize for the first time that that portion of Preston lies in a valley.

Down now past a small mall, the sun catching the stained glass in a shop window, and then I'm in front of the Enriched Bread Artists building. Starting in 1924 the bread of life was indeed made and distributed here, then the business went stale and remained empty until, in 1991, a young artist stood on her boyfriend's shoulders and peered in, and in her imagination saw an artist's collective rising up as the dough had once done. Now it's a reality, a warren of creativity and paint splashes, and one of the highlights of the Nuit Blanche, the dusk till dawn arts parade run in September.

Over the O-Train tracks, past the great flat box of the city works complex, and here is another industrial building given over to the arts, The Gladstone Theatre, originally a garage, then the home of the Great Canadian Theatre Company from 1982, in whose seats I laughed and cried many a time. It is still a cozy commercial theatre, under different and perhaps less earnest management since 2007. And then I am alongside Preston, where the smell of coffee and cooking and car exhaust overwhelms the traces of canine urine in the snow-banks.

There is no denying the colourfulness, the playfulness of the large, multi-faceted act of sculpture that takes up, no, let's say occupies, the northeast corner of Gladstone and Preston. Entitled "Bambini" its first impression is of a bowling theme, complete with pins and balls. As the name implies, it is actually dedicated to children and meant to represent how a child might sketch a soccer team. Like every piece of public art this one, funded by local business and created by Chantal Gaudet, raises eyebrows, causes headshakes or rolled eyes or smiles. The weather is lousy today, cold wind and icy pellets in the air, but it will be interesting to see how the children of Little Italy take to it in warm sunshine.

I sit on one of the Bambini balls contemplating the view eastwards and the old line about "I could make piles sitting here" comes to mind. Back in the 1870s the stretch of street I'm about to embark on lay in a part of Ottawa called Archville. Gladstone was known then as Ann Street, but lost its gender and name some time after the death of and in tribute to British Prime Minister Gladstone who died in 1894. (Ann was the wife of Thomas McKay, the rich master stonemason on the canal project. In other words, she was a local.)

Across the street from the Bambini, behind a hedge, a snow-covered soccer field bears no track of cleated boots, but come Spring, in this World Cup year, the field will fill with sliding tackles and shouts. As I rise up the hill, I come level with the Adult High School, and indeed many schoolers of adult appearance are scurrying along the edges of the building or heading for a nearby café. The building, which formerly housed the High School of Commerce, was considered highly modern at the time it opened in 1967, complete with its very own IBM computer the size of a moving truck. Now it looks as though it belongs in a Cronenberg 70s sci-fi movie.

The pointy, clean façade of St. Anthony's church seems to block Gladstone's progress, but the road dekes left around it and the street's character drops back half a century. There are car lots, the sales prices hung in the windshield hidden behind a veil of snowflakes, and small Italianate diners advertising espresso machine repairs, and single houses clinging on to the side walk awaiting the tide of gentrification to come and wash them away.

I pass a violinmaker operating out of a small Queen Anne style home, then a brief outpost of Chinatown on the north side, then at the intersection with Bell Street I look up at the battlements of the eponymous apartments to see they are getting a face lift. Some of the oldest apartments in the city, they were and may still well be student dominated affordable housing, and nicknamed Peyton Place.

In need of central heating and a treat, I slip into the Pressed Café, the vanguard establishment in a digestive changeover that has started up in this part of Gladstone, similar to the one well underway on Somerset. Patrons leave healthier than they arrived, and live music breaks out at night and samples of zine writing are available in a rack by the washroom door, none of them more than four dollars.

I take up an observation post in the large front window. A man on the opposite corner, with no gloves, using a stick and smoking, coughs loudly, and then a mini-van slides to halt by him and he stumbles into it. As the van pulls away the pre-smart phone-age children come out for recess into the playground of Cambridge Street public school, dressed in neon-coloured snow-suits. A gang of them assembles in the corner nearest to me. They drop to their knees in a circle and some ritual with a box takes place in the circle's centre. One of them scoops up a handful of snow and chews it, and I am back in the schoolyard at Vincent Massey, looking down in the snow at my front teeth, knocked out by an ice ball.

As I resume the walk, something strange is happening in the sky. The sun is breaking through, the snow has stopped and the whole mood of the street has changed; it shifts gear and my fellow pedestrians raise their heads. At Bronson I look back the way I have come and get a sense of something missing. There was a large house here on the south side, covered in a hue of yellow that required sunglasses. It was called the Pawnderosa, and at one point had become so covered in graffiti that the City ordered a cleanup. Since the building was due for demolition in a matter of months, the owners gave the City the bird by painting it the colour of sunshine. It lasted that way for several years. Now there is a bland gray row of town houses under construction in its place. So it goes.

One of the several pleasures of walking about Ottawa imbued with an ever-increasing—but never complete—history of the city is the sense of being in two tenses at once. It is a bifocal mental state, the internal equivalent of those photographs appearing on the Interweb lately which show, say, present day King Edward and then allow you to swipe back the top photograph to reveal beneath the exact same aspect but taken fifty, a hundred years ago.

Were you to attempt that photo trick with the stretch of Gladstone between Bronson and Bank, favouring the south side, the first impression would be that the two pictures were much the same. In fact, I don't believe there is another ribbon of road in Ottawa that has remained so steady in profile. Originally a residential street along its length, what businesses there are now, and there are many, have moved into and customized the single homes and kept the street in a two-storey world. The only uplift in the roofline comes near Bank, where a low-rise, stone clad and tastefully-fitted apartment block on the north side— doorman-worthy entrance, elegant balcony railings and Art Deco lamps—graces the street and is of a sort with buildings elsewhere on Kent.

On the north corner at Bronson sits McNabb Park, which bears a sign saying "This park adopted by the McNabb Neighbourhood Improvement Bunch." Opposite, the long brown terraced row on the south side reaching all the way from Bronson to Bay could easily make a backdrop in a '50s movie, and if one of the doors opened and a man and a woman emerged, he wearing a fedora, she too a hat and their respective coats of camel and fur it would seem apropos. Or a hundred or so years ago they may have been crossing the street to watch a hockey game at Dey's Arena, which sat a block west of where the McNabb arena is now.

The Dey family was prominent in Ottawa society, owners of a boat business that served the lumber industry. They were hockey players themselves and instrumental in the public advance of the game to the fever pitch level of today. They started with a natural rink where the ugly DND headquarters now squats by the canal. Then, when the railway went in, they shifted sites and in 1896 built a proper arena on Gladstone, possible the first custom-built hockey arena in Canada, complete with bleachers and a press box. That rink lasted until 1920, when fire got it. By then it had hosted several legendary games, including the first Stanley Cup win by the Ottawa Hockey Club in 1903; the famous 1905 challenge of Dawson City against the Ottawa Silver Seven, and the 1906 championship playoffs final game between Ottawa and the Montreal Wanderers, which the *Toronto Globe* at the time labelled "the greatest game of hockey ever played on Canadian ice, or any other."

Proceeding eastward from the McNabb arena, within which a game is always in progress, it is not until you focus on the details that the infiltration of the twenty-first century into the streetscape becomes apparent. A small sandwich board offers "laptops from $99," and a corner store can kit you out with digital surveillance equipment, when you want to spy on yourself and give your government a break. Meanwhile, several stores make play with the historic aspect of the street; one of the two barber shops, both sporting Canada-colours rotating poles, has covered its windows with blown up photographs of old-world barbershops. (The other shave-and-cut parlour advertises itself as open seven days a week. Remarkable.) Even the master tailor at the eastern end has loaded his window with, for some reason, old home movie equipment and bygone tailoring paraphernalia. Many more stores and businesses seem impervious to time; Majestic Cleaners, for instance, has been there on the corner as long as I remember, as has Dominion Radiator. There is even a resident clairvoyant, who would be delighted to use the Tarot cards to help you if you had "Questions that needed Answers."

Those outcrops of modernity that do appear are by no means obtrusive. The setback strip malls are discrete, and a lawyering firm is neatly packed into what appears to be a converted garage. Drawn by the smell of cooking, I step into a plain food emporium that is most modern in its marketing, and prices, but the food is, by nature of being largely organic and local, nutritionally akin to your grandmother's diet, i.e. before Big Food began turning us all into chemical reservoirs. By contrast, a store down the road is offering ostrich and emeau (sic). A permanent recorder installed in one of the bus stops along here would catch the multiplication of languages spoken on the street since the arena burnt down, and would include a rising percentage of Arabic. An aural history of Ottawa; there's an idea.

On the same side, further down, sits a photographic studio, the oldest standing building on the block, built in 1910 as a livery for the Alexandria, the famous hotel founded by Thomas Babin. By 1923 it had become Horner Motor Sales, one of the first automobile showrooms in the city. In the mid Thirties, it was the home of Progressive Printers and was heavily reinforced to hold huge presses on the second floor. The building is so solid that it once easily withstood a car crashing in the front window.

At 391, with a cornerstone dated 1911, very near to Bank, opposite the side-by-side music stores that offer daily renditions of the intro to *Stairway to Heaven* or a Cockburn tune from neophyte rockers and folkies upgrading their instruments, is a red brick building offered for lease. The stained glass windows are brightly African in design, but in fact it was once the Salvation Army's Gladstone Community Church, which closed for asbestos removal and other repairs in 2011 and was consequently put up for sale instead of being reoccupied. It was purchased by Tony Q, a local parking lot operator who buys and restores heritage buildings.

Muddy water on my boots and snow on my toque, I line myself up at the corner of Gladstone and Bank to puddle hop between there and Cartier, where Gladstone ends. The Bank-Gladstone intersection is flanked on its east side by two buildings erected in what henceforth I'll call the Banal Style, a style with which Ottawa is littered. The northern building is a box of an ex-bank, while the southern is an uninspired condo with a drug mart wedged into the bottom, complete with an entrance supported by their trademark ugly concrete pillars. Both buildings are the triumphs of lack of imagination or will to add any ocular interest to the cityscape.

The south side, in its journey to O'Connor, consists of a brilliant, almost Mediterranean single-dwelling renovation followed by several body houses, by which I mean buildings devoted to, in turn, yoga, massage therapy, yoga and a funereal business that has buried our dead for eighty-eight years, one that I have sadly and inevitably had to attend several times, as the roll call of the city gradually turns over. The funerals of luminaries such as Pierre Trudeau and Jack Layton were arranged within. An addition to the older funeral parlour carries a City plaque complimenting the taste with which it was designed, and rightly so.

The north side of the avenue thereafter, as I approach Metcalfe and pass O'Connor, seems to consist entirely of a row of garages and open space for parking. I make an excursion onto Frank, one street north, to check out the front of the houses relevant to these garages and discover wonderful brick, ornate mansions, now sub-divided into apartments, showing a brave face and a shabby backside, their gardens stolen by the car.

East of Metcalfe, Gladstone hosts the side of a '30s apartment block (the Trafalgar) and the frontage of a twin pair of similar blocks, the Gladmore and the Bessborough that give this section some class. The Art Deco doorways and chevroned panels between floors are part of the woefully short stock of Deco that Ottawa has. In complete contrast, on the opposite side, there is a beige, stuccoed building, previously unnoticed, that must surely now haunt its designer; a '60s blight that would make a lovely anything else. One of the city's major developers has its name on the door.

Outside the Bessborough I run into an acquaintance, a young man from the neighbourhood much given to cycling, who informs me that the pothole situation on several parts of Gladstone is among the worst in the city. In fact, beginning last year and ending in this, Gladstone from Bank to Cartier will enjoy a makeover above and below ground, with wider sidewalks, resurfacing, more trees and safer cycling.

The final stretch of Gladstone, running from Elgin to Cartier, is of a gentler, narrower disposition. St. Luke's park runs the length of the north side, a proper urban city park with tennis courts, a heritage field house named after a family deeply associated with the park, the Bethels, and much ado for kids. The park is on the original site of a hospital, St. Luke's, which was torn down and buried in the 1930s. Things are mostly residential on the south side, a couple of steps down from the grandeur of the Frank Street houses, and interrupted by an electricity sub-station with small print warnings on a side gate about the possibility of killing yourself if you go in. And thus Gladstone ends at the intersection with Cartier, after a close to four-kilometre run from Parkdale. It is a busy, mostly old-fashioned sort of a street that begins with a church and ends in a park, and does a lot of business in between.

King Edward Avenue

Postcard of King Edward in better days, looking south towards Rideau.

*W*hen I gaze upon archival (by which I mean pre-motor-car) photographs of King Edward Avenue, or the postcard of the avenue I have from the late-1800s, I sigh. There is not an eighteen-wheeler lane-eater in sight; the trees are reaching for each other across the boulevard. There is an air of life ambling along rather than rushing.

Standing at the north end of King Edward outside the back door of Maison Sophia, the red brick temporary reception centre for refugees, the view southward is testimony to the motorized vehicle's ability to ugly up the urban streetscape wherever it rolls. A smoking trio of refugees squatting on the concrete at the side of the centre are shouting to make themselves heard above the trucks blasting by, and their Doppler descending din is audible all the way down to Rideau Street.

Six lanes away, on the other side of the street, is a small, triangular, tantalizing park. It's on the banks of the last stretch of the Rideau River before it decants into the Ottawa. There's no one in the park today, despite the balmy, cloudless weather. Add a greenhouse coffee shop, a few picnic tables and a path by the river, and the place would be full. The ruined stone pedestals of the bridge that once ferried the railway from Lowertown into New Edinburgh are still visible in the water. Bridges come and go slowly in this tri-river town.

This stretch of King Edward, in Ottawa's earlier days, was just called King Street. An offshoot of the Rideau Canal, the By Wash, crossed it linking it to the Rideau River proper. When it was prettied up and the wash filled in in the late 1800s, it was renamed after the reigning monarch, Edward VII, the one who waited a heck of a long time for his mother to vacate the throne. Nowadays King Edward is in transition again although it seems to be taking forever to finish it. At the moment it's a twin line of residences and services, none more than four stories high, with a commuting and trucking thoroughfare vivisecting it. I can see some new Parisian-style lampposts, some recently planted, fume-choked trees and not a bench in sight. It's a very unwalkable stretch of town, with little in the way of those pleasing oddities—a mail box made out of skateboards, the odd plastic owl and some Maple Leaf flag curtains, that make it walkable. (There are mini-billboards all along the street with government propaganda on them about "Investing in Cultural Spaces" and a website you can go to, where finding out anything useful would take you all day; I gladly gave up after ten minutes. Many better things to do.)

King Edward's character is defined, for the most part, by the ongoing lives of our poorer neighbours, anchored by the good people of the Shepherds of Good Hope and the Hope Housing Complex at the Murray Street intersection. At least here they grace the street with human presence, with evidence of life in all its variety. There are some interesting individual homes along the way, a Baptist church with its fine-looking Sunday congregation lighting up the street; city-run services and businesses such as an Aikido school, a Thai restaurant, a lawyer who can help you consolidate your credit. Communal pride of appearance is a virtue that has gotten into other streets in Lowertown, but almost any strip of asphalt where big trucks are the top of the food chain, that street tends to give in, commerce trumping culture to the detriment of the face of the place.

Heading south from the refugee centre on the west side, the first numbered house is 84, testimony to the fact that the street once extended north. A block of apartments with a young couple in the process of moving out is next, friends waddling in and out with furniture. The first building of architectural note is a redbrick little fortress, bearing the name Armand Page in white faded letters on the side facing King Edward. An insert on the front wall states it was built in 1897, and there was a fire chief with that name in the Sixties. It was originally the Number 5 Fire Station, and now is privately owned.

The first historic brass plaque on a wall doesn't turn up until numbers 174/176. It's a stone double pair of cottages, which probably indicates canal stonemasons were the first occupants. Directly across, on the east side at number 175, is another stone building with a plaque, the ex-Stoney Hotel, built in 1866 as a grocery store and renovated as apartments in 1999. It's actually the best building on the street, to my mind, worthy of Quebec City. Back on the west side there is a functioning corner store, open till eleven, called the Nile Grocery, run by Debalke and Abby who are from the Blue Nile portion of Ethiopia and took it over thirteen years ago. The stone theme continues on this side at the York Street corner, where J. P. Laurin has been providing

Monuments of Distinction since 1900; the blank tombstones sit in the sunshine in the yard awaiting signatures and messages. I recall some of the more infamous tombstone messages, like the English comedian Spike Milligan, who had *I Told You I was Sick* carved on his.

A row of boarded-up houses awaits demolition on the east side, where once the porches were full of chatter by those with dining reservations at the Shepherds of Good Hope that night, and the guys and gals working the traffic lights with their baseball caps sat counting the day's take.

Next there is a wonderful line of buildings. It starts with the Champagne Public Baths and Fitness Centre, Ottawa's first municipal swimming pool and one of the first indoor pools in Canada. Originally the structure was built for the greater hygiene of the working-class residents of the neighbourhood, many of who had no baths in their homes. The structure was also originally home to a library. Work began on the building in 1921 and it was completed in 1924 with, until 1967, separate ground level entrances for each sex. The building, a blend of the Spanish Colonial Revival and Prairie Styles, was designed by Werner Ernst Noffke and was named after Ottawa mayor Napoléon Champagne. The pool was also unusual in that it was salt water, which meant it did not need to be chlorinated. It was soon followed by its sister Plant Bath on the western side of town. While popular for many years, usage declined as the facility aged. In the 1980s, after the completion of the newer Le Patro facility, the city proposed closing the Bath. After public protest it was decided to renovate the Bath at the cost of some two million dollars. The transformed facility opened in 1990.

A little further along is the cultural space that is the La Nouvelle Scène francophone theatre, housed in the old Caplan warehouse from 1920, then the No. 4 Ottawa Hydro Electric substation, which would make a wonderful local art gallery/ café if it is ever turned off, and then a francophone Seventh Day Adventist church, housed in a red-and-yellow-brick keep with economy-sized minarets. The whole row—there is even some green space in between for those who enjoy afternoon al fresco cocktails—has a smile-inducing eccentricity that could be the saving of the street if it was allowed to breed its way northward.

And then here is the corner with Rideau, with the plain ramparts of Constitution House on the east side with soldiers coming out of side doors, a secretive government building like the redbrick one set back on the west side at number 350 which has signs in front warning you not to loiter. Or else what? Waiting at the lights to cross over to the east side, where a spiffy LCBO does a bubbly trade, a young woman in a hoodie announces to us all that it is her twenty-seventh birthday; she's off to get some happy juice. The light changes, and she says, "Come on boys, there's a good time awaiting over there."

After King Edward crosses Rideau Street, and we get past the 24-hour gas station where the cashier offsets his midnight ennui by chatting up Ottawa U students, and the boring-box Quality Inn with its ground floor Don Cherry hostelry that presumably shows replays of hockey fights on its big screens, the road begins to rise up. It ascends a hill that was once fairly sandy, hence the name of the district we're entering—Sandy Hill. Côte-de-Sable.

It might well, had history run differently, have been called Bessererville. The trick to colonization is to get there first, and Louis-Théodore Besserer, who fought in the war of 1812-1814, did just that when he was granted a great whack of land on this hill, which had already been de-treed by the time he got there in 1845. Louis built his own mansion on the east side at number 149 King Edward, and it is still there, darkened by traffic fumes but holding its own. Besserer subdivided his real estate treasure trove, laying out blocks in an east-west Georgian grid to the north of Laurier, and in a north-south pattern to the south of it. The Besserer mansion passed onto William McDougall, a father of Confederation, in 1860, Canada's first minister of public works. McDougall was turned away by Louis Riel, no less, when he tried to enter Rupert's Land in 1869 as its Lieutenant Governor apparent.

There's a lot of stone on this stretch, enough of it in churches and houses to show that this was once a prospering strip in an upmarket part of town, the place Catholic money aspired to hang its chapeau, as well as a selection from the higher rungs of the bilingual federal civil service, which was just getting going when Besserer died in 1861. For quite a while it was Ottawa's swankiest neighbourhood, a legacy that has left Sandy Hill with the best collection of architecture, certainly the most warmly walkable, to be found in town.

On the western side, after the Don Cherry sporting house, sits the Ottawa Little Theatre. Its modern premises are admirably serviceable now, but until 1970, when a fire, cause unknown, claimed it, it was a grand sort of a place indeed. It is Canada's longest-running community theatre, founded by a women's group, and thus a point of civic pride. A young Adam Beach trod the boards there, as did Rich Little. When La Nouvelle Scène moved in down the street, I had hopes that a theatre district was taking shape down here, but so far that has not come to pass—not yet.

Directly on the other side of the street is the old but lovingly restored deep-red Bell Building, to my mind the finest classic office block we have in our civic stock, up there with Central Chambers on Elgin. It's beautifully proportioned with a fitting chandeliered entrance, built back when Bell had a different sort of reputation to reflect. (The Diefenbunker would be more corporately appropriate now.) A pity it can't be lifted up and put somewhere where its elegance could shine and raise the surrounding tone.

Inbetween the two churches on the western side—St. Alban the Martyr with its centenary stone put there in 1967, while the saint himself was martyred in Britain in June, 209, and St. Paul's Lutheran, founded by German speakers in 1874—there is what looks to be an ill-treated heritage house. It suffers from two sad wings, added on like carbuncles, marring its handsomeness. According to the signs it is due to come down and be replaced by a youth theatre. Just kidding; it's going to be condominiums, of course, or what the sign calls, "spirited urban flats." (Do moonlighting, self-loathing poets write these little catch phrases that developers use to describe their projects?) And then there is Gora's Antiques.

I have a game I play while walking our streets, which is to spot the buildings that are in fact fronts for various mafias and high-end-profit trades like arms dealing and sex and drugs and such. I have to confess that I had my suspicions in that direction about Gora's Antiques, which resides in a dark Hitchcockian house, and even has a broken window flanking the doorway. The house had the last laugh, however, when I stepped into the doorway to get out of a thunderstorm and protect my notes, and turned my head to see, through the door panel window, an honest antique importing emporium! So much for the over-fertile imagination.

Facing Gora's on the east side, the less well-heeled get a rent break in the two streamlined low-rise apartments that I would date from the late-40s, and which have two Art Deco entrances and ironwork, geometric balconies that are architectural candy to my eyes.

The subsequent portion of King Edward runs out on the eastern flank with one of the prettiest rows of houses in the city, a heritage district beginning with the superbly maintained Linden Terrace and ending with a bed and breakfast that already has daffodils and tulips in flower out front. They are set back a house width, and boast a continuous roofline that seems to strive for one of every sort of architectural gimcrack, and have proper how-do-you-do entrances and summer-night porches.

Whereas this stretch started with a gas station and a hotel, it ends at Laurier in better form with the busy number thirteen firestation and, on the northeast corner, the stone mansion Panet House. Lieutenant Colonel Hon. Charles-Eugène Panet, a lawyer and a deputy minister in the 1870s, needed a big house, as he managed to marry three times and have sixteen children. It is now the gated Embassy of Angola, which rite of ambassadorial passage has befallen many a grand home in Sandy Hill. The cell-phoning Ottawa U students, passing by on their way to classes on the education plantation that is Ottawa U, barely give it a look.

My own university days, as I happily recall, involved a lot of walking between things, between classes, bars, residences, bus stops. Students in an in-between state seem to be the case here too as I maneuver my merry way southward from Laurier along the final stretch of King Edward Avenue. Of course the fashions on my fellow walkers have changed since the early-'70s —then the sexes wore roughly the same clothes; sleeves and trouser legs flared at the extremity, cloggy platformed footwear. Now it seems to be tight for women, loose-loose for men. What the sociology professors lurking nearby make of that I can only guess; mating ritual of some sort, I suppose. Everyone seems to have something in their ear.

Ottawa University has a complicated real-estate history. It got its start in Sandy Hill in 1856 when Louis Besserer donated land for the Roman Catholic College of Bytown to shift out of Lowertown. Five years later it morphed into the College of Ottawa and five years after that it got the nod in a Royal Charter from London to call itself a university. Construction of a suitably ponderous main building got going right away; that burnt down in 1903. Meanwhile work had begun on what is now Tabaret Hall. If you stand on the grass in front of Tabaret you'll notice right away it is based architecturally on the Capital building in Washington. A full century after it got the Royal charter, U of O went non-denominational and hived off the theological side of things as St. Paul's, where they continue to flourish. Along the way women were admitted in 1919, and wall by wall, house by house, the university amoeba-ed in a southeasterly direction, the path of least financial resistance.

While most of the homes on this section of King Edward bear a red U of O nameplate by the door, there are a few private homes, and they mostly resemble, as do many of the departmental homes, Monopoly houses, with some frills and a porch stuck on. There is an ecclesiastical-looking curiosity at number 545, but little variation elsewhere. All but one of what used to be row houses that were student digs are gone now. The one remaining "animal house," a white affair with the unkempt air of a feral cat declares itself with an open door, fast-food litter and a skull and crossbones curtain. I can remember when you could drive down here and see a series of cheeks hanging over balcony railings, people crushing beer cans to Massive Attack and the constant smell of charred steak on cheap Hibachis.

I walk briskly south because it has started to rain, trying to guess which university department is in which building, based on the principle that dog owners are said to resemble their dogs. The University of Ottawa Press seems nicely biblio in one of the Monopoly houses, as does the university newspaper Fulcrum, though I expected at least a hint of hash coming out a window. The math department has a nice square building at number 585, whose square root is 24.186773244895647, and the department of bilingualism resides in two houses side by side that are almost twins but not quite. The calm Muslim Prayer Centre is easily the best kept building on the street.

And then, on the west side, it goes all modern, starting with the Brookes Residence (named a touch anti-climactically after the first housing director) which since 1987 has packed in just over 700 students on streets named after two French scientists and an English saint, which is fitting. Thereafter is a see-through heating plant, the back of Colonel By Hall, and then a building that would look good in a James Bond movie, vintage Pierce Brosnan, and which is actually known by an acronym, SITE: School of Information Technology and Engineering.

Over on the east things stay funky, starting with the Fathers and Sons Restaurant, where a large screen greets you, ads for upcoming televised boxing matches adorn the windows and a trio of grey-haired professors sit at the bar calmly ignoring the late-afternoon mating rituals and discussion of the Senators playoff chances. (I pop into a nearby second-hand bookstore at this point to dry off, where the gentleman informs me that "nobody reads much anymore.") A couple of other eateries, some modern, rather dainty housing, and then a grassy field due for development followed by the Sports Complex, a building that is the triumph of function over form, where, despite the rain, a game of Frisbee played by large people is in progress on the artificial turf.

The end of King Edward's reign through Sandy Hill comes to an ignominious termination at Mann Avenue. Thereafter is a wasteland of grass, cars, buses and flyovers, which come to think of it is much how the street began.

312 Laurier Avenue East

312 Laurier Avenue East

*C*ertain buildings in Ottawa seem to act as witnesses to the evolving character of our city. As they continue over the decades to evade the wrecking ball, they host a diverse roll call of occupants, and develop a multiple, architectural personality, layered over time into the fabric of the building.

At the invitation of Bonnie, who was for many years an executive assistant with Amnesty International, I was able to tour their Ottawa headquarters, which are located at 312 Laurier Avenue East. The stately HQ has clearly been someone's mansion once upon a time, a handsome family home for someone with accumulated wealth. It's faced in golden brick with four half-circle, two-storey abutments; one each either side of the serious entrance, and one on each side, and topped off with a variety of peaked roofs large and small. Left and right ground floor covered verandas are easily populated in the imagination with Edwardian Ottawans.

Within the dedicated staff of Amnesty go about their vital business in a collective of offices large and small, some with sealed ornate fireplaces, some with high ceilings and curved window casements. There are outbreaks of fine woodwork in some rooms, and the entrance and stairs enjoy splendid carvings. The doorway has a mosaic floor. It's an architectural glory.

Amnesty has been in there since 2002, the year they bought the building from the St. John Ambulance, for which it served as their National Office. That was 312's purpose when I lived nearby, when it was called St. John House. I felt somehow safe knowing that I could run there whenever I wounded myself.

That had been its name since 1978, when the military finally moved out after occupying the place for 36 years. In the summer of 1942, a month before the Dieppe raid, 312 became the Number 12 Barracks, and the Canadian Women's Army Corps moved their duffle bags in. At war's end the Women's Corps was disbanded and 312 was turned into apartments for military men. The Provost Corps—the military police—joined them at the beginning of the Fifties, and the cell they had installed for naughty soldiers is still there in the basement. It is a storage space for Amnesty now, which is almost poetic.

The military commandeered 312 in 1942 from the Grey Nuns, the Sisters of the Immaculate Conception who, true to their name, had acquired the building in 1930 (it had been vacant for three years prior, with a sole policeman in residence) and christened it

Immaculata College. It was actually more of a dorm for the Sisters who did their teaching elsewhere, but there were some classes held there. The mansion's lineage gets a little complicated here as we move back out of living memory. The name on the deed before the Grey Nuns was the H. F. McLachlin Estate, which is a family name that historians of Arnprior will recognize, as it was H. F.'s father, lumber baron Daniel McLachlin, who was a founder of the town. H. F. and his large extended family had moved into 312 in 1909, probably as a lobbyist for his dad, who had built his first mill at the Chaudière in 1837. Among his other business appointments, H. F. was a director of the Bank of Ottawa, the lumberman's bank of choice, which was established in 1874 and issued its own currency.

Hugh Frederick McLachlin died in 1912, the year the Union train station was built, and his wife Mary stayed on in 312 until 1920, when she sold it to a sub-set of the Knights of Columbus, who sold it back to the mortgage holders, the McLachlin estate, for $1 plus outstanding taxes in 1927. Then the three vacant years, then the nuns.

And, in the beginning, Hugh McLachlin bought the house from George Goodwin. George had had the money to build the house handed to him by his uncle James, a rich railway contractor who died in 1883. George, also a building contractor, had his company build the splendid house in 1900. At the time he was a widower with five teenage kids and a brace of unmarried sisters to shelter. And that is why 312 is known today as Goodwin House, although it was only that for nine years. And before the house was built? Believe it or not the land was part of Colonel By's estate. So, from canal builder to railwayman, to lumberman to knights to nuns to soldiers to first-aiders to injustice fighters. Quite the story.

Major's Hill Park

Major's Hill park, top left. Note streetcar on its way to Hull.

I'm standing next to Colonel By, and we are both looking west and down. Down into the ravine that houses the Rideau Canal lock system he designed, and the stone building that was his HQ during the construction. By is on a pedestal, a black faceless statue, and I am in Major's Hill Park, along with a modest, scattered cast of others who have temporarily swapped the grey of the streets and offices for the grass and greenery on a mid-week sunny day in Ottawa's oldest park.

You can judge a city by its parks, their frequency, their varying design and maintenance. Running through my head are happy-hour videos of times past spent in parks; singing *Imagine* in Central Park by John Lennon's memorial; listening to Jane Siberry by the river opposite the old Ottawa City Hall; diving the marine park at Tadoussac; using the playground swings in sight of Gehry's Guggenheim in Bilbao; getting slowly over-refreshed in the Tivoli in Copenhagen; pinching myself on a bench near La Biennale garden in Venice; reading a book I'd bought at Shakespeare and Company in the Jardin du Luxembourg in Paris; feeling sorry for the belugas in the Stanley Park aquarium; eating lunch in Green Park in London while researching a book; sipping a strong tea in Regent Gardens in Edinburgh after a visit to the National Gallery. And thousands of tourists around the world must have Major's Hill Park on their memory lists. It deserves to be.

I had set out to stroll along St. Patrick, but found myself pulled instead by the flowerbeds and green slopes just beyond the Peacekeeping Memorial and Jim Hart's stirring *Three Watchmen* sculpture. A landscape architect once said to me that "Parks are where cities go to think," and I believe he meant thinking in a subjective way. Parks are urban oases, where you can slip off the clock and step into nature's rhythm. Daily half-hour walks in Major's Hill should be compulsory for all nearby politicians and financiers.

Turning away from the statue of the man described as "Ottawa's Founding Father," (which makes his wife, Esther, the Founding Mother) I skirt the fence preventing me from falling into the ravine, heading north. Every ten feet or so I have to detour around a photo op, and am only once requested to "Could you just…?" and, click, an Ottawa photo-moment is digitally frozen. Pesky bushes prevent me getting a full view upriver, but then a balcony with a marbled boat with a history lesson on its flank appears. The view upriver is heartlifting. The text on the boat's side uses the phrase "Westminster in the wilderness" to describe young Ottawa, which I have not heard before. I use a mental eraser to take away all the human doings in the view and see it for a moment as a pausing animal might have long ago; the unceasing bass thrum of the Chaudière falls filling the air. Then I turn my head towards downtown Ottawa to take in what humans have done with the site in the past 250 years. Subjective thinking.

I stand for a moment inside the foundation outline of By's house, which burnt down in 1848, fourteen years after he returned to England, his job here well done and the English treasury unjustly with its knickers in a twist over his over-expenditure. The site was excavated in 1973 and among the treasures unearthed is the By family's very chamber pot, bronzed and set on display on a low pedestal! Colonel By shat here?

Passing the quartet of picnic tables that must be frequently painted over to mask the latest crop of etched graffiti—"I LOVE LORRAINE" is the latest addition—I rediscover Hamilton Mac-Carthy's 1918 statue of a kneeling Anishinabeg hunter, the one that used to crouch at the feet of Samuel de Champlain on Nepean Point. His view of the river has been much reduced by the relocation. Nearby a squat, stone maintenance building is begging to be turned into a hot brown beverage room with some more picnic benches out front. I must say, however, that the park is superbly benched, with the wood and metal variety, none of those gauche plastic jobs. A work crew is repairing a stone wall here, an echo of the Rideau canal construction days.

The grassy open middle ground, where once the city frolicked in May during the Tulip Festival, is largely unoccupied, except for a band of gentlemen from the Mission, seated in a circle discussing low finance, their shirts off and their tattoos on show. There used to be a young man in a wheelchair here who would fly a kite everyday using a fishing rod and line to pay it out, but he is elsewhere today. I walk over to the corner of the park near the Connaught Building, my eyes down to avoid having to see the American Embassy/fortress.

Public art is a love it/hate it affair, but I like the "wooden spiral weather vane thing," as it is self-described that sits near the Mackenzie entrance. It's called *Twist 1.5*, dates from 1978, and sums up for me our historical affinity with the surrounding forest and our exploitation of it.

Mackenzie Avenue

Mackenzie Avenue, 1938.

I'm looking at an old black and white photograph of Mackenzie Avenue, just before I walk down its short length, heading north towards the National Gallery. Were I to step into this 1938 snapshot, the first thing I would notice is the relative tranquility. As with just about everywhere else in Ottawa, there is a frenetic air to contemporary Mackenzie, construction bollards stretching off on both sides as far as I can see. In the photograph, once past the two large buildings on the corner at Rideau—the Chateau Laurier and the Daly Building as was—there is only cleared space on either side. Not so now. In the photo, one can see why Lady Aberdeen had plans for this to be a ceremonial drive, not a commuter bottleneck.

In fact, there are only five buildings on Mackenzie, all of them large, representing two countries. On my left is the east side of the Chateau Laurier, which has been there since 1912. On my right is a glassed-in bit of terrace attached to a restaurant which is in its turn part of a high-income condo at 700 Sussex, an NCC-owned stone-clad miscast building, that I have dubbed a prison wing for rich people. The grandeur and detail of the copper-roofed Chateau shows up this unimaginative block across the road, each building representative of the architectural attitudes of their eras.

Walking down the east side, to avoid the sidewalk reconstruction outside the Chateau, I pass a set of stairs and an elevator down to Sussex and then stand in the forecourt of the Connaught Building, which is full of government offices. The large wooden doors on this side actually access the third floor of this castle. Construction began during the First World War and was completed after Armistice. Look at it for a while, and it may remind you of the Museum of Nature; it should, because the two buildings share the same architect, David Ewart, a man who favoured the Baronial style; the Mint is also one of his.

And so, past the wonderful, American designed, York Street Steps, to the American Embassy. A Janus-like building, with its modern black glass and vaguely Art Deco entrance towards Parliament Hill, and its more traditional stone side towards the Byward Market. There was a raft of objections to the building being put where it is, back in 1999. There was its view-blocking potential, which is valid. And the inevitable disruption to the heart of Canada's capital, also valid, because we have lost two lanes of our traffic system. (Apparently not; a fortified bike lane is in the works for part of the lost lane on Mackenzie.)

Crossing over to the west side of the street at the Peacekeeping Monument, where a life-sized bronzed soldier regards me through binoculars, I can now stroll back alongside the wide,

Parisian-like sidewalk that borders Major's Hill Park, named for a Major Bolton who took over after Colonel By left. The park once hosted the blooming tulip festival celebration, and now only gets musical enhancement on Canada Day, which is a pity. At the risk of repeating myself, an annual Welcome To Ottawa festival should be held here for that year's newcomers, despite the NCC actually being the park's overlords. All too soon I'm back at the frenetic intersection of Rideau and Mackenzie. I think I'll head back to the park.

McBean Street, Richmond

A calm McBean Street, looking south from Perth Street, Richmond.

I'm standing on McBean Street, looking across at the oldest, still standing house in Richmond. Early 1820s. When this nondescript Colonial style home, first occupied by the Maguire family, was being built out of freshly felled trees, the Rideau Canal was a set of plans about to become reality. It was the building of the canal and Ottawa's subsequent rise that blocked Richmond from any chance of becoming Canada's capital, which at one time looked to be a possibility. The tranquil town of Richmond exists because the British Military, after the dust had settled on the American invasion that ended in 1814, was anxious to keep a militia of ex-soldiers around in case the Americans, or maybe just the Fenians, had another go at the world's oldest contact sport, colonization.

Four hundred soldiers and families on half-pay were duly dispatched from Quebec City under the leadership of one Colonel Burke in 1818, to make a garrison cum settlement on the Jock River (then known as the Jacques River; later Scottified). Eventually, after adventures on LeBreton Flats and road building through the forest, they began their town where they had been told and to the specs they had been issued. They survived a primary winter, grew the town and today it is the senior settlement in the present boundaries of Ottawa.

The oldest house is clapboarded now, and modestly does not have a plaque upon it declaring its heritage. None of the older Richmond buildings with a lengthy story have plaques, as far as I can tell. I head down McBean Street towards Perth Street, Richmond's main drag, and immediately cross the Jock River. The views of the winding river, its banks unspoiled, are immensely salubrious, and having that level of riverine beauty on your common doorstep must be continually beneficial for the town's general temperament.

With my antenna up for signs of early Richmond, I catch sight of a small smoke house tucked at the back of a garden, looking like a simple shed. Two men are working on a minivan in front of it, and the smoke house is casually placed in the grounds of the house that replaced Hill's Tavern, once the social hotspot of the fledgling settlement. It was on this very lot that the Duke of Richmond, the newly appointed Governor General of British North America, did not enjoy his last, as it turned out, meal. He was unwell, in fact he was rabid, having been bitten somewhere along the way by a fox. He died, terrified of water, while being canoed down the Jock River towards Quebec City.

McBean Street is the heart of old Richmond—several buildings on it were already occupied when Bytown was being built-and within a few yards of the smokehouse there is an old general store, built in 1843, the faded letters of "BIRTCH BROTHERS" still visible over a doorway. Across the street is the former Bank of Ottawa, built as another general store in 1863 and converting from apples to accounts in 1901. Several more vintage professional residences adorn McBean, getting relatively younger as you approach the end of the street. Then at the junction with Perth Street I walk over to the entrance to the Richmond Agricultural Fair Grounds, and suffer for a moment from memories of Lansdowne Park as was. The prettiest building on site is the old Town Hall, moved there from McBean Street.

After taking note of the fairgrounds, a fifteen-minute stroll gets me to the Quiet Garden at the rear of the Anglican church. Note the capitals. It is indeed a tree-lined, bench-filled oasis, a member of a worldwide organization of Quiet Gardens. The labyrinth within provides some pleasant subjective thinking time, once the lawn mower has moved on. In the graveyard behind, I visit the vault of Captain George Lyon, a Richmond pioneer and one of the founding four hundred. There is always a pioneer with the most get and go, and that was Captain George, and his wife Catherine. He is reputed to have cut down the first tree, owned a lot of the acreage, set up most of the industry and gone into politics. Two of his sons became mayors of Ottawa (hence Lyon Street.) A busy life which earned him a prime spot in the graveyard and a handsome tomb.

On the way back to Ottawa, travelling in reverse down the Richmond Road, I pass the cairn erected to commemorate the death of the Duke of Richmond. A man on a runaround lawn mower is cutting around it. A tidy memorial for an untidy death.

Metcalfe Street

Metcalfe Street looking north from Somerset Street in the 1920s.

*T*he traffic is flowing one way and the snow is funnelling the other on Metcalfe Street, as I begin rambling northward from the big wooden doorway of the Museum of Nature. Metcalfe, in its heyday, was one of Ottawa's swankier addresses—several of Ottawa's one-percent lived there—lumber barons, mayors, inventors, lawyers. It's come down a few notches since then, but the whiff of bygone wealth is still detectable here and there.

Metcalfe Street actually begins on the far side of the museum and of the Queensway, at Patterson Creek. At the end of the 19th century and the beginning of the 20th a lot of the classier buildings on the street appeared, and the southern end was part of the development of three residential mini-estates designed by Ottawa's better architects, people like W. E. Noffke, to attract the city's moneyed class. If you want a dose of real estate envy, a stroll along this southern portion of Metcalfe will do the trick. In 1905, construction began on the Victoria Memorial Museum, alongside a Canadian National Railway line and that southern segment of Metcalfe was cut off from the rest, like chopping off a piece of a worm. The severance was compounded when the Queensway replaced the railway line in 1957, and now you can't get there from here without a detour.

Crossing the forecourt of the museum, I quickly negotiate the short stretch up to Gladstone, which is a mixture of pleasant homes or home-like buildings filled with lawyers and such, and a sore-thumb apartment block on the corner with a leprechaun motif stuck to the wall. It is while waiting for the light to change that I recall whom the street was named after. Charles Theophilus Metcalfe made a career of telling colonies what to do on behalf of the British Empire, including Canada from 1843 to 1845. His main purpose while here was to keep the colony as royal as possible after a bout of rebellion.

On the other side of the lights there is a very pleasant stretch of similar but differing three-storey brick apartment blocks with an air of first-third-20th-century about them. They bear names like Trafalgar and Metcalfe Terrace and have proper entrances, including one with an Art Deco proscenium doorway that is a treat for Deco-starved enthusiasts like me.

The rather melancholy-looking Ukrainian Embassy is the first of several foreign outposts on the street; the Nigerian Embassy, a troubled place these days no doubt, with an idling RCMP van outside, is just north of the Ukrainian. Arriving in the 300s, the first samples of Ugly Modern exteriors rear up, with the polish of names such as the Grosvenor and the Executive. The house with the Virtu-Car station outside, however, is more fun, with Queen Anne wooden gables and filigree putting a brave face on it. I'm reading its historical plaque as several people with important things to do brush past. 301 Metcalfe was built in 1899 and was the home of Douglas Brymer, the first Dominion Archivist and father, it says here, of the painter William Brymer, a tutor of Group of Seven member Edwin Holgate. As our first archivist, Douglas started in 1872 in three rooms in the basement of Parliament with no staff and not one document, but stayed at it for thirty years and laid the foundation for an institution.

The Greek Temple on the opposite side, the First Church of Christ Scientist, that never seems to have anybody going in and out of the front doors during the week, has always intrigued me. I assumed it had once been a library and was subverted in use, but in fact it was custom built for the congregation and in a couple of years will be a century building. I am told that within, it has two pulpits.

Two more homes of once-important men are on this stretch; the fanciest, looking like a deluxe bouncy castle, is the former home of John Rudolphus Booth, lumber baron and real estate owner. Booth, by all accounts a stern, humourless man who started out his business in a hut by the Chaudière Falls, had his mansion built in 1909, and died in it sixteen years later at the age of 99. The house moved out of family hands in the Forties and became the Laurentian Club. I read somewhere that Booth owned enough timber-laden land to lay a mile-wide strip from coast to coast. As I often say, the trick to colonizing is to get there early.

One of Booth's neighbours when he moved in was Thomas Birkett, who by then had founded a hardware business and been mayor of Ottawa and a Member of Parliament and married the stepsister of his first wife. It was on Birkett's watch that the electric streetcars began to purr around Ottawa. His slightly more modest house was nicknamed Birkett's Castle by the good citizens of Ottawa and is now the Hungarian Embassy.

At the corner with Somerset, getting weary of squinting at plaques, I park myself briefly on the restored steps of Campbell

House, built in 1883, now the headquarters of a real estate group. (The old line about "I could make piles sitting here" again comes to mind.) Alexander Campbell was a Father of Confederation and a law partner—smart move—of Sir John A. Macdonald. He ended up in the Senate. I pass a quartet of men having a smoke outside the Labour Council office as I slip into one of the city's gastronomic landmarks which, since 1967, has the reputation of offering the town's best pizza. I imagine the quartet outside stubbing out their cigarettes and bursting into do-wop singing.

I tend to regard Somerset Street as the southern border of Upper Town, and there is a mood swing as I cross the frontier and continue northward along Metcalfe; things become more brusque and business-like. The goal of the gates of Parliament Hill, with the main building glowing like honeycomb in the crisp sunlight, is about ten blocks away and my fellow pedestrians have their shoulders hunched against the finger-numbing cold. Despite that, several are texting as they slow-motion along, and we with our gloves on walk around them.

First up there's a car park on the west side, with a box-building on the other that is buzzing with dentists, including the one that tends to my oral problems. He jokingly calls this building the House of Pain. Fixing people is a bit of a theme on this stretch of Metcalfe; there are two former gabled houses that now advertise themselves as "wellness centres."

Thereafter there is a brief flurry of low-rise apartments, beginning with the Duncannon, a splendid, winged redbrick affair from 1931 with Tudor affectations that has, according to its plaque, hosted the likes of Martha Black and Yousuf Karsh in its time. Perhaps like you I'm guilty of not knowing who Martha Black is. Turns out she is quite a story: a Chicago-born woman who went twice to the Klondike Gold Rush and made money there, and later at the age of sixty-nine was elected to Parliament, the second woman to achieve MP status. She died in 1957, and her autobiography is on my list of lives that should be made into movies.

Although there is not a plaque on the Medical Arts Building that I can see outlining its architectural history, there is one that states that "near this site" (where exactly they don't say) a gentleman called "Carbide" Willson had a home. Thomas Willson, a Canadian who moved to the States to make his fortune, worked out how to manufacture calcium carbide—needed to make acetylene—and got rich. He moved here at the very start of the 20th century, hit the social scene running and hatched wondrous expensive schemes, some of which, like the Churchill Falls Dam, later came true. Apparently he owned the first automobile in Ottawa, but I thought that was Thomas Ahearn. The Art Deco-ish, yellow-brick, Medical Arts Building was built in 1928 by W. E. Noffke, and I can see a monkey-on-its-back tower somewhere in its future.

There is a big hole in the ground on the other side from the Medical Arts Building surrounded by hoardings advertising a new condo building. The pretentious advertising that accompanies this one lets you know that it is "Redefining the Skyline," a true statement that can be taken two ways, and no prizes for which way I take it.

The northern corners of Metcalfe at Laurier hold a basket of memories for me. On the west side is our public library's main branch, and please don't judge this building by its cover, which is butt ugly. If we had stood on this corner in April 1906 it would have been packed with people celebrating the opening, by Mr. Carnegie himself, of the classical Carnegie library that the ugly one replaced in the mid-70s. I had a library card there as a boy, and went swimming Saturdays in the YMCA in the building opposite, now the Hotel Indigo, formerly the Hotel Roxborough. Later I wrote a history of the Ottawa Library, which brought me full circle. The YMCA opened in their second home (the first was on O'Connor) in 1905, and the original Senators hockey team was billeted there for a time, while Karsh lived there as well from 1930 to 1934.

By the time I reach the Sparks Street Mall crossing, past several nondescript buildings and the clever bronze statue of the native hunter taking bow and arrow-aim at a bronze stag in a nearby flower bed, I must have gone by a dozen sandwich boards squatting on the sidewalk at the bottom of tall buildings warning pedestrians that there is a Danger of Falling Ice. (There is no danger from rising ice, of course.) Call me naïve, but shouldn't people who build tall things next to the sidewalk in Ottawa the wintery city have to design them so the ice stays on the roof or is disappeared? There is one street gentleman who has been seated cross-legged on the sidewalk for many winters near the church of St. Peter and St. Paul, begging, who has defied death by icicle impalement so far; I wish him a long life.

The street ends at Wellington with a whimper on the west side, with an empty ground floor in the building where the tourist office used to be. The office, which was in an ideal spot when it was here, has been moved down the street to somewhere in the World Sexchange Plaza (sorry about that, couldn't resist), a journey I suspect not many will bother with, as all the world's facts continue to take up residence in little hand-held computers. The nearby statue of Terry Fox, with a tidy pile of snow on his head, dressed in shorts and a singlet, looks out of place in the new, bellicose Canada.

Montreal Road

Montreal Road in the early days of the motor car.

*W*hen you walk across the elegant Cummings Bridge into "Le Quartier Vanier," as it is now branded, there's a heavily treed, unoccupied island on the right-hand side, about an Olympic long jump from the bridge. It's not much of an island, but it's where the settlement of Cummings Corners, which grew into Vanier, began. Charles Cummings, no doubt known to his friends as CC, had enough money to put a general store, a blacksmith's and a carriage works on there around 1830. He also had the very basic bridge that hitherto spanned the Rideau spiffed up. You can see the stone wall of the bridge abutment at the north end of the island, rising from the shallow flowing water. It has the word ADDICT graffitied on it.

For a brief while Cummings Corners was a place for well-heeled Anglos to set up home away from the bustle of downtown Bytown—the poet Archibald Lampman took himself for creative walks around there—and after some discussion the place became known as Janeville. Several sources claim to not know why that name got pinned to it, but others are happy to record that the wife of John McArthur, a settler in Gloucester Township around the same time as Cummings, was of that name, and I'm good to go with that.

Janeville lingered beside Clandeboye (named after an ancient Irish kingdom) and Clarkston, two riverside clumps of settlement north and west of it, and then in 1909 all three were given the collective title Eastview, which was the direction from the Parliament Buildings where it lay—and still does. Eastview towned itself in 1913, citied itself in 1963 and gradually became an island of mostly francophones, surrounded entirely by the oil slick of Ottawa. When the first all-Franco-Canadian Governor-General, Georges Vanier, died amid the centenary celebrations in 1967, Eastview took his name up a couple of years later, and resisted being swallowed by Ottawa right up until the great amalgamation gulp in 2001.

There's a mural alongside the beer store in the strip mall at the corner of Montreal Road and the North River Road. It's on a wall of the delivery ramp, so it's not easy to view, but you can get the picture of Cummings Island and the bridge. (The present bridge went up in 1921—Ottawa bought Cummings Island a year later and demolished the buildings—and got done over beautifully in 1999. The team of people in Vanier who are valiantly trying to beautify the place, want flowers on the beautified bridge, in baskets, but City Hall seems to be dithering—security, theft, that kind of excuse. Just let 'em do it.)

Heading east from the end of Cummings Bridge, past the slightly sad, little chained off dismantled greenish space, there's a crying need for hanging baskets here as well. Montreal Road goes about its business in a relaxed, not to say healthily louche kind of way, and it certainly has life on it, but apart from the murals there is very little imposed gentrification. I don't think I've had more nods hello, ça vas or corner conversations anywhere else in the city. Even a gentleman talking to a very friendly beat cop while taking a liquid picnic on a bench near the community centre took a moment to wonder how I was.

The next thing that strikes you after the absence of foliage is how ethnically diverse the stores are; this stretch could easily take the name Little Everywhere. In one strip mall alone, bookended by a beer store and a movie store, an Irish pub, a Lebanese grocer, a Chinese restaurant and an African beauty salon are cheek to cheek. Back in 1975 then- mayor Bernard Grandmaître, who was actually born here (the Grandmaîtres are a political dynasty in Vanier) had plans for a row of 12-storey gleaming white apartments and a moving sidewalk no less, but not a thing came of that. Montreal Road's retail emporiums, cafés, cheque-cashing institutions, beauty salons and South American travel agent answer the neighbourhood needs and it'll take an invasion by another, higher-income tribe to change the place. And then where would everybody go?

The best way to look into Montreal Road's past is by studying the murals. They are above, just back of, and on the side of at least a dozen buildings in a half-mile strip, and they accumulate to a reasonable narrative of the Janeville-Vanier timeline. They are all signed by "Yeatman" and as murals go they are pretty good, well-researched and composed. Here is the story of the Eastview Hotel, on the same site for a hundred years before it burnt down; here are three generations of bingo players portrayed on the bingo parlour wall; here are the famous NHL-playing brothers who played road hockey on the side streets.

Crossing the Vanier Parkway (why are they oxymoronically called parkways? Runways would be better; certainly most of the drivers on them seem to be trying to take off) the murals continue and the streetscape stays much the same, apart from a very nice funeral parlour, until you come to St. Margaret's Church, just past the shiny new paramedic station at Number 200. Built in 1887, the little stone building with the cottage feel to it shows signs of a difficult upkeep now, but it was the Protestant stronghold for decades while the rest of town was mucho Catholic, and it holds services in Inuktitut once a week. The church was locked on the mid-week afternoon I was there and the XXX movie "palace" across the street was open and receiving visitors. I could stretch to a Montreal Road metaphor out of that, but I won't.

When I needed a place in Ottawa to live in 1978, fresh off the interminable bus from Toronto airport, I shared a garage-sale-furnished apartment with a family friend on Montreal Road, in a three-storey brick affair called Place des Pionniers, number 278. The place is still there, as are the petit confectionary store and adjacent coin wash on the opposite side of the street. I lived for a few months on beans and small boxes of soap powder till I got a part-time janitorial job in a day-care centre.

Then I heard nothing but French on the street and in the stores, but now, as I continue walking east down Montreal Road, there is almost as much English in the air (a fact borne out by the demographics; as of 1996 less than half the close to 25,000 Vanier residents are first-language French), and a fair bit of the French has that elegant Haitian accent. A hand-lettered sign outside the African Bamboo club announces that the System Band d'Haiti will be appearing at the end of the month.

The last thing Montreal Road is on these few blocks is quiet. The traffic noise, car and bus (the hallowed numbers 2 and 5) is constant long into the night, and the percentage of people on the sidewalk talking to themselves—or rather to someone we can't see—in a raised voice is comparable to the Byward Market. But it's always been that way on chemin Montréal; Beechwood was the original main Vanier thoroughfare, and it had a streetcar which Montreal never did, but buses have been on the street since 1923; the charge in 1927 for children under 51 inches tall was three cents. The railway used to cross where the Vanier Parkway is now, and in the Fifties, when the Eastview movie house was packing them in and bars like the Maple Leaf Tavern, which lasted seventy years until 1994 and proudly served quarts, were roaring, the street was even busier.

To compensate for all the buzz on this stretch there are not many oases of calm, which I consider an essential part of streetscape planning. As usual around Ottawa, there are not enough benches (I'm starting to sound like a broken record about this) and you wonder if a digital, non-XXX repertory cinema could make a go of it. They usually do in areas where many people are between employments or are making a living below the Revenue Canada radar.

As a reflection of the majority annual income in this part of Vanier, there are several shopping opportunities for previously-enjoyed items in the pawn shops, flea markets (one of which specializes in "biker items'), and the Salvation Army emporium in the front room of the Concorde Motel. The latter is full of "magpies" today, several perusing the books section, and everyone seems in a good mood. The Wabano Centre, the Aboriginal health centre on the north side, is a distinctly, delightfully calm place when I step in. The Wabano is on the cusp of a major expansion designed by Douglas Cardinal, and it could well become an architectural and community gem in the future. It is so easy to bury at the bottom of the garden the fact that all this civic land, including Montreal Road, has never been ceded to the occupying Europeans, and that the McArthur and the Sparks and the Cummings clans simply rode in here and tied up their horses.

From here on down to the crossroads with St. Laurent Boulevard, the street does quiet down as the Catholic church goes about its business, as it has done in earnest since August, 1887 when the Montfortains, the Sisters of Mary, settled here and got the parish of Notre-Dame going. The first real hint of the strong Catholic presence is a sign in a Fifties font on a hydro pole asking you to turn left if you are looking for the Notre-Dame de la grotte de Lourdes. The grotto is a purpose-built spiritual oasis, put there in 1908, the fiftieth anniversary of the founding of the mother grotte in France.

Next comes the rather groovy church of Notre-Dame itself, which has a sort of Flash Gordon style to it. Opposite that the Maison Accueil–Sagesse, one of those fine Catholic pieces of architecture set well back from the road that dot the city and make condo developers drool over the real estate they sit on. Then back across the street to the gates of the Notre-Dame cemetery, the nearest thing to a park this section of the road can come up with. (By the way, if the history of Vanier intrigues you, you can visit it virtually at *museoparc.ca,* a work in progress that is already one of our best neighbourhood history museums, or actually visit it in beautiful Richelieu Park.)

Rather like that *New Yorker* magazine cover that showed Manhattan, then the river and then the rest of the world in the distance, Montreal Road keeps going and going, past the Montfort hospital, one of the finest examples in the city of the triumph of community and language over tone-deaf governmental accountancy, and then further out the movie-set campus of the National Research Centre and then the road morphs into a highway and whisks you off to la vrai Montréal.

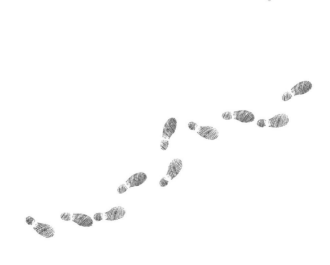

Old Barrhaven

The Jockvale school in Barrhaven, class of 1906, now a community space.

*A*mid the gusts of conversation in a downtown coffee shop I recently caught the phrase "Old Barrhaven." Looking around the room, any one of several people could have been an Old Barrhavian—how do you tell?—but the apparent oxymoron was so striking that I made note of it and wrote *"Investigate"* alongside.

Traveling down the straight-arrow Greenbank Road and heading deep south I pass a church sign that reads THE SECRET OF LIFE IS... FILL IN THE BLANK. Well, if you don't know, I don't, but at a guess I'd say it's, "Evidence of Caring." What looks to be a giant beige bug turns out to be an inflated indoor golf arena and then the car breaks free of the hem of Ottawa and there are wide, flat, fenced-in fields on either side for quite a ways. Ominous looking concrete structures with many chimneys and checkpoints are dotted at odd places in the fields. Government research facilities, I'd imagine. Possibly agricultural.

Another roadside sign, a green-blue one on Greenbank Road as I cross the Greenbelt, announces my arrival in Barrhaven. Underneath the town name are two words. WELCOME HOME. Ahead a town rises as a line of houses on the horizon, as though the horizon itself had been planted with home-seeds tightly packed into a bed and they had all sprouted. (Please note that at no point in this article so far has there been any word play at the expense of Barrhaven.)

After blipping my brakes a couple of times to aggravate the tailgater I've collected, in the hopes of bursting her blood pressure, I cross a road with the lovely rural name of Fallowfield and turn left onto Larkin. Some stores, a pub, and as I cross Tripp, here I am, in Old Barrhaven.

When a fellow called Jacques Gréber did a redesign number on Ottawa in the late 1940s, his first set of blueprints suggested the idea of satellite towns the other side of a greenbelt. These were to be towns that were in Ottawa's orbit but were pretty much unto themselves, striving to be self-sustaining. The descendants of that idea are Orléans and Barrhaven, which are not as Gréber envisioned them; had they turned out as he planned for, there would be no daily commutation to Ottawa.

Back when Ottawa wasn't much more than dirt roads, lumbermen and ex-canal workers, the land to the south was farmland, and farming families with names like Kennedy and Quinlan and Neil (notice the country of origin theme emerging here) and other represented nationalities opened the fields and grew produce to feed the growing conurbation above them. Times slowly changed, and in the 1960s developers began to fulfill Gréber's call—sort of. The fields began to grow houses.

Old Barrhaven now is a well-settled looking place, nestled in among newer Barrhaven's more uniform sections. Blink and you could imagine yourself in Alta Vista, lots of twin-garaged bungalows, no sidewalks, block-long continuous front lawns that the English find so unprivate. The bushes still have those little sandwich boards protecting them from winter, but a few mobile basketball hoops have been set out at the end of the drive. I see no-one walking, indeed I feel no compunction to get out of the car myself, and drift past two schools separated by a soggy looking park, the rink boards still up, then up a hill, and back onto Fallowfield. The internal combustion, Philip Glass car-symphony is constant here and all the houses that back onto the road have tall solid fences behind which lie empty swimming pools. Soon the final school bell will ring and the noise of kids homeward will compete with the traffic.

Before embarking for Old Barrhaven, I had read a short online memoir by Mike, who was born there in the late 1960s. Though he could see Ottawa in the distance, Mike considered his childhood a small-town upbringing. You met everybody in McIntosh's grocery store, at least until the mini-mall came in and there was quickie pizza and fried rice to be had for dinner, and after school you could slip into the remnant forest and go through the junk piles and hunt for gooey frog's eggs. There were rumours of an old Indian trail and arrow heads to be found. There was the winter carnival and the summer Field Days, with a soapbox derby down Larkin Hill. Now the population of Barrhaven is approaching one hundred thousand and counting; counting rapidly.

Leaving Old Barrhaven behind, a brief drive down to Strandherd (a street name that conjures up pictures of cows on the loose) past seemingly endless consumer opportunities, interspersed with drive-through what-evers, and then a right turn has me on the lookout for the old schoolhouse Mike's memoir had mentioned and indeed, here it is, a classic, with the date 1906 over the doorway. It is now a museum. An old yellow farmhouse with actual gables and a wood porch sits next door, looking like a senior citizen at a rave.

I try the schoolhouse door. Locked. I can see desks in a classroom and then notice a timetable taped to the inside; listed on it are five prayer times, from Fajr at six in the morning till Isha at nine-thirty at night. The museum doubles as a mosque. Old and new Canada in one building, sharing.

Returning to the car I notice a big-box electronics store across the street and submit to the consumer itch. With four lanes between me and it I decide to shun the car and walk over. I take up position on the side of the road and wait for a gap in the traffic. There isn't one in sight.

Old Orléans

St-Joseph Boulevard, 1970. Today, Place d'Orléans is on the left.

*D*uring a chance encounter with an acquaintance a few weeks back, I was admonished for only writing about a small part of Ottawa, roughly the downtown square mile or two. "How about Orléans, where I live?" he gently challenged me. "What's the matter—scared?"

I knew not much about the town, I had to admit, based on no more than a handful of hit and run excursions there. The abiding myth of the place for those of us who are ignorant of its charms was that it had sprung up fully formed from beneath farm fields sometime in the early Eighties. At its heart was a huge consumer cathedral, and every weekday morning almost everyone who lived there got in their cars and headed for Ottawa, returning eight hours later. A few people were left behind to run the place till everybody got safely home, which most of them did. Avoiding the highway, I take the Rockcliffe/ Aviation parkway to its end, wondering again as I proceed why on earth they didn't put the War Museum out here, meanwhile renewing my vow to visit by canoe the scattering of unoccupied islands in the Ottawa River someday. Then left-turn onto St. Joseph. I have decided to discover old Orléans, such as it might be, and do not have to drive far before I pass a quite lovely old stone house. Turning the car around in a gateway I realize I have U-turned in the entrance to a fenced RCMP compound. Now they have my license plate, and redaction to Wawa cannot be far away.

The lovely home turns out to have a plaque at the entrance, announcing it at the top as the Butler House, and then tells me that the first occupants were the Tierneys—the Butlers came later—and that the building dates from the early 1800s. How early it doesn't say. The place had a major reno in 1998, and it looks idyllic. It had been a resting place for dust-covered travellers in the horse-carriage years after Montreal Road opened up in 1850. One of those rural Eastern Canada movies they don't make any more could easily be set here.

There is a fruit stand next door, and on the pretence of buying a punnet of carrots I engage the stand's proprietor on the history of the farm behind the stand. His French is far superior to mine, since he is French-speaking, like the majority of his fellow Orléans residents, although the percentage has declined in recent years. So we speak in a mélange of both official languages, a very east Ottawa thing to do. The farm was once the property, he believes, of the Oblate Brothers, the White Fathers, the same ones who started Ottawa University, and they came out here to grow food for themselves and their academic flock. "It's very Catholic ici," Paul says, and indeed it mirrors Canada, in that the French got here first, the Church ran the place, and then marauding commercialism and the English language elbowed its way in.

Not much further towards the epicentre of Orléans, I pass another, slightly larger stone house of equal antiquity. The plaque on this one is better informed, and lets me know that in 1855 the Grey Nuns bought 500 acres out here to provide food for the mother house and it became known as the Youville Farm. By the 1880s, it had become a religious community, and held the distinction of being the best dairy farm in the province. It also did time as a village school, then a convalescent home, and is now partially occupied by lawyers. Ain't it the way.

Walking down St. Joseph from the Youville Farm building, I return to the modern world of cheek to cheek, owner-occupied, small retail stores, each advertising their own niche, interrupted most often by something to do with cars. The spire of a large church beckons, standing out, as it does, like a sore divine digit. Pausing outside to take in the grandeur of Paroisse St-Joseph d'Orléans, the rain begins to fall heavily so I scurry into the office, which has a reassuring 1950s feel to it, and I'm quickly handed, by a very genteel lady, a history of the parish, produced on its 150th anniversary in 2010. From this I was able to draw a succinct history of the town, as follows.

Orléans's first settler was English, one John McKinley. Then came François Dupuis, who had served in the war of 1812. Next Joseph Laflamme who by 1825 had cleared five acres, and built a mill. Even as late as 1946, as an aerial photo shows, it was really no more than a crossroads. It was a police village for 51 years, right up to 1974, and then it took off like a booster rocket and now is the eastern wing of greater Ottawa. Just a few doors down from the church there's a piercing parlour and an adult movie store. I decide to conclude my mini-tour of old Orléans by rooting around for historical nuggets in the local library.

I turn up Edgar Brault Avenue, named after the man who started the volunteer fire service in 1946 and, after many a turn, all of which seemed to bring me back to a street labelled Dufour, I find the library and bellow out a cheer of triumph. And a pleasant library it is too, the ghost of the word Gloucester above its entrance and old beams within. I'm shown to the small section on local history on a lower shelf, and dig in. There were two scant pages in one thin book, a history prepared by students. They put even money on the theory that the town was either named by its first post master, Théodore Besserer, who was ancestrally connected with the Ile d'Orléans, or a hotel and store keeper, Luc Major, who drew a kitchen table map of the area in the 1850s and registered the name Orléans, his wife's ancestral home town. The students also included the crash of a CF-100 plane in 1956 into a residence, killing fifteen people.

The clock, as it does when I get to researching flies around the dial. Walking back, I can hear the rumble and rev of the commuting cars that are trying to get home on the nearby clogged highway. I'm not in Old Orléans anymore.

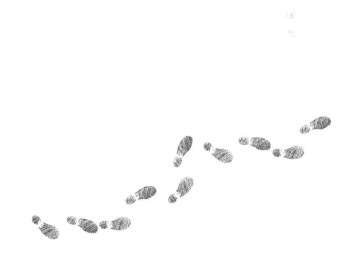

Preston Street

One of the *Postcards from the Piazzas* artworks lined along Preston.

*E*nterprising Italians have been coming across the Atlantic to Canada for over five hundred years, ever since Giovanni Caboto, a Venetian hired out to the English, made the crossing and, without asking local permission, claimed the east coast of Newfoundland for his employer.

Thousands more made the trip of a lifetime in the following centuries and, unlike Caboto, they settled here; some as decommissioned mercenaries in the Eastern Townships in the late 1600s, others after serving in the War of 1812-14, then in Montreal in the early decades of the 19th century, where the streets filled with busking tenors. Likewise in Toronto. By 1901 there were eleven thousand Canadians who could refer to a town or village in Italy as their starting point.

Here in Ottawa, a late-starting city between the two bigger Italianate centres, the streets around the north-south bisector that is Preston Street filled up with mostly southern Italians, in a big way in the years before the First World War and again in substantial numbers for a decade or two after 1950. As is the North American habit, this area was duly labeled Little Italy, and there are signs on the road bridge half way along Preston and the recently erected, rather basic arch at the southern end to reinforce the area's heritage.

There is, however, little sign at the northern end of Preston Street, the end nearest the Ottawa River, that a Little Italy lies to the south. The fact that the street bears an English name doesn't help. There was a brief false fact floating around a little while back that the street was named after one Isabella Preston, a famous horticulturalist and hybrid lily creator who came to work at the Experimental Farm in 1920, but the more mundane truth is that it carries the surname of George Honey Preston, a city councillor from all the way back in 1858 and again in 1860. George was a shoemonger by trade. Certainly the street had been Preston-ed by 1894, according to the wonderful historic map of Ottawa by Karl Baedeker.

The streetscape at this end is looking pretty good these days, having been disrupted for quite a while. The theme for the street fixtures is a burnished, galvanized metal that frames the bus stop shelters, the semi-Parisian, low-slung street lamps and the waste bins and, oh happy day, there are plenty of attractive metal benches on most of the widened corners, including one outside the corner store at Elm that today is occupied by two men in mid-discussion of the sorry state of the world in general, both performing some neat manual Italianate choreography.

After passing a well-treed and gardened row of the backs of the housing units that begins Preston, there are several tenement rows of older buildings as I pass the various intersections with what I collectively call the tree streets—Primrose, Elm, Spruce and so on. The houses have been a little crumpled and bumped by the years, but they are all graced with a sheet-sized front garden, every one of them well maintained. It doesn't take much in the way of tidy horticulture to boost the charm of a street.

And now the commercial stretch of the street begins, just before it intersects with Somerset. On the west side, there is a neighbourhood pub called, well, Pubwell's, which enjoys a tavern atmosphere but does not sell beer in quarts. There is a well-known local poet/writer at his station at the window corner table, note pad open and a selection of books on the round wooden table. Every pub should have one. Next to that some people are coming out of a fresh pasta store with full plastic bags.

I climb the marble steps of Luciano's Fine Foods and I'm assailed by the aroma of cheese and sausage. In no time I am chatting with Mr. Luciano himself, who asks me to, per favore, drop the mister. His family came over in 1952 when he was a teenager, and he opened the store in 1963, first in the building on the present site of Pubwell's, and then here, two doors south. Over the years, he tells me as he leans against an aisle-end of biscotti and the like, he has injected but two principles into the business; quality and service, and thus he remains open. Teenagers who worked for him at weekends now come in to stock up for impending parental visits. Stores such as Luciano's are the tent pegs of a community.

Still on my quest to make it to the corner with Somerset I run into Mimmo, the local barber, sweeping the sidewalk outside his two-chair shop. And great chairs they are too, from the Fifties, the streamlined kind; I begin plotting a midnight raid to purloin one until I notice how well anchored they are, able to withstand great weights being lowered into them. "My father opened here in 1972, and I think it might well have been a barber's before that." We discuss the empty lot opposite his store, which has been that way for several years. It was occupied, it seems, by Tender Touch Massage, one of Ottawa's first such establishments; its workers would sometimes treat the young Mimmo, stationed outside his father's shop, to a glimpse of a grown woman in a nightie enjoying a cigarette. The Tender Touch burnt down, which didn't upset too many local residents, and according to a billboard on the site it is the intended home of a museum dedicated to the Vietnamese Boat People; a step up indeed.

With memories of dismal scalpings at the barber's when I was a schoolboy dancing in my head, I proceed to the intersection and wait for the light to change. Across the street a young woman is filching redeemable empty beer and soda cans out of a small hedge.

At the pedestrian crossing the illuminated striding white man permits me to bypass the road works on Somerset—there is an epidemic of street surgery this summer—and I grab a bench in front of the Plant Bath. In the small park, in front of the baths, a life-size statue of a Vietnamese pieta, a mother and child, is hastening both away from and towards something and is dedicated to *Those Who Have Lost Their Lives in the Quest for Freedom.*

A recent wreath standing in front of the statue says it is from Vietnamese communities in Montreal, Toronto, Calgary, California and Sherbrooke. Chinatown (or rather Asia Town as it probably should be called now) braids into Little Italy at this point, as witnessed by the little store opposite, which is a purveyor of *"Bubble Tea, Cappuccino and Vietnamese Sub."*

The two entrance doors of the original Plant Bath building are closed now, though the etched word *Spectators* remains above one, and it's true; we are all spectators these days. The bath was built in 1924 (as was the Champagne Bath on King Edward) in a wave of hygienic concern by the well-to-do of Ottawa for the well-being of the less-well-to-do of Ottawa. It's named not for horticultural reasons but for the mayor at the time. It was drained and closed in 1990, and nearly went the way of all heritage in Ottawa, but a tidal wave of community spirit saved it, and it was extended and much improved, and now stands proud and popular. It was mid-afternoon when I was there, and all the lanes were occupied by goggled, (not Googled) locals indulging the queen of fitness sports.

If there's one theme running through this section of Preston Street, apart from the fact that it is a serious eat-street, suitable for a gastro-crawl, it's weddings. They are everywhere you look; a photographic studio has some arty images of a happily hitched couple shot from above, as they kiss against a wall. Another window is stuffed with multi-tiered white cakes that you are just dying to grab and playfully push in a friend's face. (Remaining on the subject of food, surely it is now possible for absolutely everyone in Ottawa to go out one night of the year and find a table somewhere?) Elsewhere you can have a video made of the happy day. I used to joke that marriage is a great institution, but who wants to live in an institution. I wouldn't crack that one in a café down here.

The other theme of an equal weight on Preston is soccer. There's a park with two pitches right alongside the Plant Bath. As if to confirm the impression a little brother walking with his big brother goes past me with RONALDO on his back, who is actually Portuguese but never mind. (If you do not know who Ronaldo is, there is no hope for you.) Further down the road on the east side is another field where I once saw two teams consisting entirely of men with grey hair playing. When Italy won the World Cup 2006, the street went ball-istic.

Further down, on both sides of the street there are several low concrete pedestals set at intervals, as though waiting for streetlights or some such to be mounted on them. In fact, their true purpose has recently been revealed this week—they are the supports for a public art project by the Wakefield artist cj fleury, who has a knack for likeable and impressive public art, not an easy trick to pull off. Her works of public art, to be fully installed within the month, consists of fifteen "Postcards from the Piazzas"; they are chess piece-like works of bronze and granite. Art as history, history as art, and the one already up is both pleasing and appropriate. No street should be without its own art.

At the corner of Gladstone, where if I turn my head I can see the parish church of St. Anthony's one street over to the east, miraculously lit and glistening in the midst of a sun shower, sits Preston Hardware, the store of choice for Little Italy's picklers and preservers. The store is doing a brisk trade in such paraphernalia right now, as the back garden tomato crop comes in, and there is nowhere else in town I can get bits for the old wooden handled tools and ratchety things I pick up in garage sales.

Preston Street is likely to have a festival at the drop of a tenor. The Ferrari festival, I'm afraid, has just roared off, but La Vendemmia is coming up. It's a harvest-time celebration of food and wine, and both staples of Italian life will be in even more generous supply than usual, and there will be a charity grape stomp on the Sunday. Now, where else in Ottawa would you get to witness that?

One of the side effects of the building of the Queensway was a series of terrifically ugly underpasses strung east-west across the city like vertebrae. One such tunnel appeared halfway down Preston when the Queensway chewed into Little Italy. These concrete tunnels, which would serve as ideal film locations for scenes from slasher movies or horror flick portals to hell, are the very definition of banal.

Most neighbourhoods ignore them and leave them as is, while the graffiti artists, the knights of bright, use them as concrete canvases. But Little Italy has used theirs as a sort of Bayeux tapestry of Preston Street's history. The artist Karole Marois, in 2007, created a tableaux of Italian-ness that makes walking through the tunnel, towards the light at the end, a reasonable pleasure, not to say an education. En passant we learn that between 1945 and 1965

250,000 Italians immigrated to Canada, most of them arriving at Pier 21 in Halifax. There are silhouettes of hatted men and skirted women bearing luggage towards a better future at street level, and running above are portraits of the more-well-known businesses and families of Little Italy. It almost succeeds in making the underpass attractive. I'd suggest large screens showing works of art or webcams to famous global landmarks or upcoming cultural events—and no exterior advertising, which I view as landscape pollution —as a solution in other tunnels.

It being midday, I step into the Prescott Hotel and fearlessly order a meatball sandwich con frites und coleslaw, as advertised in neon italic in the window. The room contains many men and not many women, and no less than a dozen TV screens of various sizes showing a variety of sporting events. No one is paying the TVs any attention until a fight involving several hockey players beating up on a fan who had invaded the ice comes up, and all heads swivel to the nearest screen. While waiting for my meal, I read of the history of the place from the cover of the menu. Anthony Disipio opened a hotel on the same spot as a Purveyor of Beer and Wines in 1934, renamed it as the Prescott in 1941, and went from strength to strength, pushing the eccentric squareness of its pizzas. And it still has internal phone booths, which is a remarkable act of survival.

The spreading, warren-like empire of the Pub Italia continues to thrive on the opposite side, complete with its beer paraphernalia store window wherein a crass sign informs me that beer has been helping ugly people have sex since 1862. Presumably they either didn't have sex before then or they didn't need any help. I check the clientele inside to see if any of them were using beer as a pimping agent, but it is difficult to tell without prolonged study.

Thereafter Preston Street thrives as a sort of vast banquet hall divided up into separate cells that are its restaurants, including what must be the thinnest restaurant in Ottawa, Il Piccolino. This strip from the Queensway down to Dow's Lake is not as homogeneous as it once was—there are Turkish, Indian and Irish bastions now, and the first really bad looking modern unimaginative building, apart from the Bank of Nova Scotia, has appeared as part of a complex that houses two hi-tech towers—but you can still find modest, happily scruffy homes leavened into the mix, a garage or two and even a Thai boxing gym, where I would have liked to put a foot in the door but it was closed for business, although I doubt they have been kicked out.

It is unfortunate that the first building on Preston Street one encounters if entering from the southern end is a bank, not only that, a drive-through bank. When western civilization finally does collapse, one omen historians will seize on that was ignored at the time will be the drive-through bank. Next we have a Lutheran church, and the rudimentary arch advertising Little Italy links the two. Ottawa is not big on historical arches; Maybe we will see a few more archways around town in future, perhaps one at the entrance to Rockcliffe with "Little Anglo-Saxony" written on it.

The Preston arch, which dates from 2002, is part of the fairly recent application of "destination" theory to Preston Street, a modern aspect of the science of tourism which converts cheerfully self-satisfied areas of the city into destinations people will want to return to once they have been there, usually to eat out and stroll and spend money. Often there is an unfortunate Disney-esque outcome when streets try this, and the sense when you visit these "destinations" that you are being milked rather than catered to, but Preston Street has avoided this. Sitting on one of the benches at a widened corner, watching the Prestonites at work and play, is a fine way to pass on hour—make that two.

Promenade du Portage

Rue Principale in 1920, now Promenade du Portage.
Note the streetcar lines.

*T*here was many a late night, in the 1980s, when the taverns and juke joints both along and just off Promenade du Portage in Hull were full of Ottawan bar staff. They were there to grab an extra hour or so of revelry, because the more puritan Ottawa called a halt to alcoholic consumption (and subsequent behaviour) at one in the morning. Catholic Hull carried on for an extra two hours but when the Ontario government gave in and extended the daily drinking hours by one, the nightly caravan to Hull dwindled.

The terrible architectural carnage wreaked on the Hull waterfront in the late Seventies and early Eighties as part of Pierre Trudeau's honourable bilingualism mission begins at 1 Promenade du Portage, along the stale faceless front of the red-brick Terrasses de la Chaudière. In those glory days in the last century smokers puffing away indoors were enthusiastic and legal, but now they have been shown the door, and there are permanent clusters of them outside the entrances, inhaling hard and discussing the latest cock-up.

In a small park in front of the Terrace I find a monument to the farmer, lumberman and colonialist Philemon Wright (he was American, from Woburn, Massachusetts), the founder of Wrightville, which begat Hull, which begat Gatineau. Erected in 1950, it marks the 150th year after Wright emigrated here with a small band of settlers and kick-started the National Capital Region. In 1806, Wright steered a log raft down the Ottawa all the way to Quebec, and launched the timber trade here. The rest is pulp.

There are hoardings up on the north side after Promenade crosses Eddy. A high-rise financial tower with a glass prow is in mid-construction behind them, dwarfing the poor old boarded up Bank Hotel with its photographs of '40s Hull affixed beside the front door. The Promenade proper starts with the old Bank of Montreal on the southeast corner with Eddy, until recently a pawnshop, now a pizzeria. The Wright family held the deeds to the land for over a century; it was a home, a hotel and as of 1907 a bank, servicing the savings of the lumber workers. All that's left of the word Montreal over the doorway is NTREAL, or "not real"; what that signifies I'm not quite sure; perhaps something to do with bank profits. Like many other older buildings on the promenade, it dates from after the Great Fire of 1900, which started in Hull on

April 26th and wiped out almost all the buildings on the street. The essential ingredient in any enjoyable streetscape capable of supporting life is a variable roofline, preferably coming in at under five stories. This is the case for most of the north side of the Promenade (a word that evokes the characteristic of being pleasant to walk down) and about half of the south side. The non-governmental buildings on Portage have variable rooflines in spades, with dormers, fancy brick colonnades from the late Twenties, and some tinwork at the top that would look good in Paris. Their cumulative effect is not entirely destroyed by the traitorous greyness of the Portage Complex at the east end, which looks like it was designed in five minutes on an Etch-a-Sketch. Standing in front of it, I realize that it's the row of homogeneous storefronts at the bottom of these monsters that drag down the vivacity of any street. Ottawa has dozens of them, with more to come.

The nickname for the streets around Promenade was once Le Petit Chicago, a name it earned from its bootlegging activities during Prohibition, which began during World War I. Al Capone visited and avoided paying tax here—or so the story goes. During the big band era the likes of Louis Armstrong played just down the road at the corner with Montcalm at the Standish Hall, formerly E. B. Eddy's house. While I stand here outside a club that carries the name Le Petit Chicago, checking the band posters, a young man passes me in a singlet and shorts, in true Canadian defiance of the temperature. He goes in, and I realize, from his mugshot on the poster on the doorway, he's a musician. Probably not a bootlegger.

There is a church on the street, St. James, or rather there was. In the mid-'80s St. James was the compassionate heart of downtown Hull, with AA meetings and daily mass at noon for civil servants. It opened its doors a century earlier in 1886, and sufficient of the walls survived the Great Fire that it was quickly rebuilt. Now it stands empty and unmarked, a sign of the times. What to do with closed churches is always a puzzle (they make great music venues) but their preservation as architecture is essential. They may soon be all that's left to stop the condo and office towers banging into each other, in the same way that articles in newspapers stop the adverts from colliding.

Next to the church these days is a parking lot, but I happen to know, because someone who used to live there told me, that for sixty years or so there were homes here, a redbrick side-by-side triplex wherein the children would fall asleep to the carillon of the church. Next to that was the Lemire music store, with sheet music in the window and Gisèle MacKenzie album covers. One magical day, television sets appeared in the window and the street kids got their first look at a very small black and white Uncle Chichimus on a screen about the same size as an iPad.

Almost opposite the church, at number 119, there is now a training school for hi-techers, but if there is one building on Portage I would love to see revert to its former glory it is this one. From many years after 1937 when it opened with the movie *One in a Million*, this was an Art Deco cinema palace—the Cartier. Okay, I've mentioned the Art Deco deficit in the region already, but a digital cinema with a Deco façade might draw people here at night. The city shut it down and bought it in 1991 after it had gone into a taste tailspin, but in its time it was a shining beacon. To give them credit, when it was renovated they restored the Art Deco fin over the doorway, and it catches the eye as the old Strand Art Deco cinema does in Montreal.

The grandest extant building on the street for me is the "fine home" of Aubry House at number 177, doubtless built with the intention of holding that title. The Aubry in question was the mayor of Hull around the turn of the 19th century, which made him the man who had to handle the resurrection of the street after the Great Fire. The neat trick of the house is that it has twin front facades at right angles to each other, one being the mirror image of the other.

A left turn after Aubry House (the only building on the street with a historic plaque) past the old freestanding clock takes me into the courtyard where the true bacchanalian fun took place when I was an habitué of the nightlife here. The Bop and the

Bistro (now restored, and nicely restored at that, after a minor fire in 2003), the B and B as we called it, were adjacent houses of repute, ill and otherwise, and the scene of countless morning-after stories. Several of those tales surround the departed true bluesman Back Alley John, with whom a very young Sue Foley used to sit in.

The old neon Le Bop sign is still up on the wall, but DJs with names like Bouda and Casper now provide the music of a night, and the chemical (not on the premises of course) intake has mutated. It all feels somehow cleaner back here now, and more expensive, but that may be just my perception, running the red lights on memory lane.

Coming out of the courtyard, the old Chez Henri, a Renaissance mansion of a place that could have been the setting for a ghost movie starring a French woman in black, has, after many years vacant, had major reconstructive surgery on its right-hand side. The exterior (the inside isn't open yet), is a not wholly successful melding of old and new, but I've seen worse. Judges and such stayed here when it was a grand hotel, opened during the U.S. Prohibition in 1929 by the aptly named, renowned chef Henri Burger. It may well be that the phrase "sober as a judge" started here.

Rideau Street

"Rush hour" on Rideau Street in the 1940s.

I wasn't sure where Rideau Street began until I looked it up. The Chateau Laurier, outside of which I'm standing now, is 1 Rideau, so that's it. My intention is to walk Rideau Street bi-focally, one eye on the past, one on the present. Of all the downtown streets Rideau, which connects the canal of the same name to the eponymous river, is a bellwether for the way Ottawa has evolved.

A plaque on one of the Chateau's pillars explains that the Loire Valley style edifice took three years to build, at the request of the Grand Trunk Railway (later the good old CN), presumably for passengers with grand trunks. It opened in 1912, and the trains ran right smack downtown instead of inconveniently to the edge as they do now. The plaque is anxious to tell me that R. B. Bennett, not a particularly nice prime minister, lived here in the Thirties. Of course, one must here mention Chateau inhabitant Yousuf Karsh, several of whose black and white portraits of the famous are currently on display in the alleyway connecting George and York Streets, as well as within the Chateau itself.

Just as the Chateau kicks off the northern odd-numbered buildings on Rideau, the former Union Station commences the evens on the southern side. The place has the echo of the steam age, but is deathly quiet. Remarkably, there is a vertical slab of the Berlin wall, with excellent graffiti on it, in the foyer, plopped down in 1990. I ask the security guy if I can step into the main hall for old times sake, (I came in and out of this station as a boy) but no, a conference is in progress. The sandwich board at the door states that the "Multinational Small Arms and Ammunition Group" are having a symposium in there. Oh dear. Your tax dollars at work.

Heading east, I drop down into the infamous underpass, scene of the fatal stabbing of the homeless, far too young, Steven Beriault, who tagged as Cactus, on the night of June 14, 2006. It's a grim few feet of tunnel, designed by an urban planner in need of re-education about the virtues of natural illumination and elegance. A seated banjo busker gets a toonie from me for novelty, and the habitual trestle tables laden with jewelry are set out. Coming up out of the dingy light, I see they have put up three puffy cream angel torsos on pedestals, representing Faith, Hope and Charity. I like it; the more public art the better.

Across one of Ottawa's busiest corners lies the entrance to the Rideau Centre. It cuts into the former Transportation Building at 10 Rideau Street, a pleasant Gothic revival / Chicago school tower, built in 1916 by C. Jackson Booth, who had the luck in life to be the son of lumber baron John Rodolphus Booth. Rodolphus—a name due for a comeback? Ottawa's City Hall on the corner of Sparks Street burnt down in 1931, and this building was Ottawa's temporary HQ for over twenty years. The Feds nabbed it in 1965, and it underwent a reno in the early-'80s, since which the province has done provincial-type things in it. Along the way, several of Ottawa's better poets, people like Archibald Lampman, worked in here; there may be one in there still, forging haiku memos to keep herself amused.

Fairly quickly after the estimable Colonel By built the canal, Rideau Street struck out eastward and became a shopping mall, accessorized with sewers, sidewalks and gas lamps in a four-year stretch between 1850 and 1854. Three decades later the era of the all-in-one multi-floored department stores began with the arrival in 1889 of T. Lindsay and Company. Others followed, stretching clear through from Rideau to George. A. J. Freiman's, founded in 1918 and which my mother dragged me round as a boy, was the biggest. Old man Freiman was the object, among others, of a sordid piece of Ottawa history in the 1930s, when Jean Tissot, an Ottawa police officer, tried to rally some wacko local Christians to boycott Jewish businesses, Freiman's in particular. Freiman sued Tissot for libel, won, and that particular bout of anti-semitism died away. The company was acquired by the monolithic Hudson's Bay Company (known in the North as "Here Before Christ') in 1972. The Freiman Mall a little east of the Bay is testimony to the venerable retailer.

The massively ugly Rideau Centre, built in a style I've dubbed *nouveau acquisio*, dominates the south side, where once there was a row of smaller family owned stores such as Bill Ginn's photographic shop which had been on the street, in various locations, since 1959. I well remember the Centre opening, and realizing it resembled a giant playpen for consumers of all ages, cash at the bottom and platinum credit cards on the third floor. I quickly make for the carbon-monoxidy fresh air.

I'm noticing, as I make my way east down this obstacle course of people shopping and catching buses, an absence of benches, probably because if you are sitting on one you're not shopping. Ottawa is, in my estimation, a few thousand benches short. If there was one here, I'd take a break, but as it is, I'll lean on this bollard.

Over on the north side of Rideau, at the corner with Dalhousie, stands what used to be the Windsor Smoke Shop, a name that now seems almost medieval. But it was the place to go for a Halloween mask. Nowadays a mere clone convenience store, it has far less personality. Directly across the street is one of the better renovations in Ottawa, performed by the imaginative architect Barry Padolsky. The Mercury Centre has a long and honourable history stretching almost a century. It was the original RCMP headquarters, believe it or not, and then it was transformed into the Laroque Building, in its day the only francophone department store in town, which closed in 1970. The building twiddled its thumbs until 1990, when it was given an excellent make over. Quite sensibly, there is a company within it that does historical research. Incidentally, the Mercury Centre takes its name from the weathervane atop it, which depicts that god of commerce; the vane formerly sat atop an insurance building demolished in 1898. It's been spinning in the wind for 120 years, and seen a lot of changes.

The stretch down to Cumberland from here on both sides has come to feel these days, say in the last ten years, a little like lower St. Catherine Street in Montreal did a few years ago. The telltale marks of this are lots of small stores with signs announcing that an ATM lurks within, no trees set in the sidewalk (actually the whole street is desperately under-foliated) chain stores devoted to DVD rentals, second-hand CD stores, retail outlets generally catering to the more tattooed and pierced portion of the population. But then it has always been sort of like that down here. Back in the Seventies and Eighties, the north side of the street was a music strip, and I spent a fair number of my evenings in The Black Swan, Molly Maguire's, and Friends and Company soaking up raw, loud Canadian music, gulping down smoke and quarts like they were going out of style, which they were.

Returning to the south side, I spy through a window a comfortable chair and head in, finding myself in the presentation centre (new-speak for sales office) of yet another condo eating up the daylight around the Byward Market, at the same time bringing well-to-do folks downtown. I notice an advert that says the new building will be a place where "The excitement knows no bounds", which I looked for and couldn't find; my excitement remained distinctly bounded. Interestingly, and it's a parable in a way for the evolution of Ottawa, there was originally a convent here, with a chapel designed by an architect-priest; now an endangered species, I would imagine. The convent went under the bulldozer in 1972, but not before the chapel, in 4,000 indexed pieces, was saved and stored till 1988, when it was installed as a work of art in the National Gallery. Those of you wise enough to have taken in Janet Cardiff's musical glory *Forty-Part Motet* in the chapel will have an idea of what the music in Nirvana will sound like.

Then, as Sylvie, the woman working in the presentation centre with whom I have fallen into enjoyable conversation, and who lined up as a girl at the Rideau Theatre to get tickets to see the Rolling Stones, kindly points out, the convent became the Hayloft, the first restaurant in town where I heard that great cultural phenomenon, waiters singing happy birthday to a customer. So, convent, restaurant, high-rise condo in succession. From godliness to worldliness.

It is only here, as I cross to the north side, that I stumble on the first piece of public art on the street. There is an alley running between Rideau and George here, coming out opposite the Sally Ann; it's called the Waller Mall. At either end are works by artist-about-town Justin Wonnacott, in the form of large metal roses embedded in the concrete of the pathway. The work incorporates quotes from a surveyor's diary way back in 1826, the year Ottawa got started.

Standing to the side of Wonnacott's work at the Rideau street end, I click on the fact that our streets themselves are works of public art, and that we view them that way, hoping in our hearts for beauty to raise the collective mood and rarely getting it. Maybe a few artists and historians on the planning committees of city hall would not go amiss.

And then, still heavy in thought, on to the corner of King Edward, past the great survivor Dworkin Furs (the store closed in 2012, aged 111), my ears fill with the airbrakes of giant trucks, and the shouts of artists/labourers wearing hardhats and heavy orange vests, doing a prolonged performance piece of street enhancement.

Looking now down Rideau Street eastwards from the corner of King Edward, on my way to the splendid Cummings Bridge, the line of time-darkened wooden poles supporting the hydro lines appears like a diminishing series of exclamation marks.

Several concerned citizens have contacted me singling out the continued existence of these street poles as "backward," "unsightly" and so on. One eloquent citizen thinks that the poles "lurch down our major East-West thoroughfare like drunken sailors on shore leave." Another said that burying the lines and losing the poles "would prove to be the single most effective way of improving the overall appearance of our in so many ways gracious National Capital." I'm sure a citywide poll on the poles would come out against them. The cost of removing them would be huge of course, but disappearing them would certainly improve the civic visuals, as planners call them. All in good time, I would imagine.

Passing the music store on the south side where, yes, the sound of an electric guitar playing a Neil Young break is wafting out, I look into the window at Nate's Deli. In 1969, after the restaurant had been open almost ten years, John Lennon and Yoko Ono stopped in for some smoked fish. Politicians both legendary and obscure have their pictures on the wall, but soon the walls will be tumbling, when the building's new owner levels the place and something else goes up. Change is the only certainty, it seems, except in the case of the Rideau Bakery, and even that used to be on the other side of the street, back when kosher doughnuts were two for five cents.

I don't know how many hours I've spent in the Bytowne, but added together it would amount to a half-life. The building opened as the Nelson, in 1947, with close to a thousand seats, 25 cents to see a movie, and there is a minimal hint of streamlining in the exterior brickwork. With a fun, pokey little bookstore next door it's a cultural oasis, one of the few in downtown capable of generating a line-up.

And then, set back from the street, here's the Rideau Branch of the Ottawa Public Library, which actually isn't a Carnegie library, though it feels a bit that way. (The original main library was, as is the branch at Rosemount.) Opened in 1934 by Prime Minister Borden, it was designed by John P. MacLaren who also gave us the Mayfair Theatre and the First Church of Christ, Scientist on Metcalfe. MacLaren's design is a combo of French and British architecture, which is appropriate for the location. Inside, there is quite a bunch of Ottawa art on the walls, worth a look as a break from staring at the computer screens.

Not too far along, at the corner with Chapel, there is a building that speaks to a significant part of Ottawa history. 151 Chapel was the original Jewish Community Centre, built in 1951, and it was home to that community's archives until just a few years ago. Half the building now is called, poetically, Heartwood House, and it is a good place, devoted to administering compassion and education. Moses Bilsky was our first Jewish settler, who came here in 1858, within months of it becoming the capital, although it took more than a century for Ottawa to get its first Jewish mayor. Hopefully in another century or less we will have our first Muslim in the big chair.

Most of the still-standing, single-dwelling homes on this stretch of Rideau have been co-opted for commercial purposes, mostly food, from organic cafés to burgers and Chinese-to-go, to an upmarket emporium in an old house with porch dining, no less. There is a distinct oddity at the beginning of the 500-block, a driving school. The row of three ex-residencies, still with their wooden gables, opposite the superstore where *Le Droit* used to be, has evolved into what will some day hopefully be called Little Africa. There are enough stores there and thereabouts that have gone Afro to make the appellation worthy.

Meanwhile, there are still residencies here and there whose tenacious occupants get to hear the rush-hour cacophony twice a day. The brick duplex at 531, flanked by some decent single-storey stores, is wonderful and even has a small front garden. Further down, just before the end of the street on the south side, are five homes, no two alike, that speak of the once upon a time of the eastern end of the street. One gets the sense that, if it wanted to, the portion of Rideau from King Edward eas could go the way of the Wellington/Richmond boulevard, and why not? We could do much worse, and have.

And now here, on the north side at number 589, is one of my favourite renovations in town. I call it the Armoury, and it once did serve that purpose, but it is officially Wallis House and was built in 1873 as a Protestant hospital, back when people got sick according to their religious denomination. Then it switched sides to become a Catholic Seminary, and then the military moved in, in the shape of the WRENs and then the armoury. It is now a unique, stylish apartment block.

Sticking to the north side, as I come level with the yellow Romanian Embassy, the road curves down to the Cummings Bridge and there is a brief, very pleasant view of the rooftops and trees of Vanier, appearing for a moment almost New Englandish in the Fall daylight. The bridge is an historic cultural dividing line, by which I mean it is a *bridge* one end and a *pont* the other. In one of the little balconies the bridge provides I pause and look down at the Rideau River. Rivers are the ideal metaphor for Time, and in the current there is a piece of driftwood moving rapidly northward.

Scott and Albert Streets

Scott looking east, 1960s. Tunney's Pasture would be built on the left.

he cars are tip-toeing through the intersection, heaters on max and wipers in a frenzy, as the winter storm sets in. It's the intersection of a street named after an Ottawa mayor, Scott, and an English bulldog statesman — Churchill. Back when Westboro was the centre of Nepean Township, Churchill was the Main Street. This crossroads is the starting point for an expeditionary trudge along Scott Street and onto Albert, all the way to Elgin.

In fact, there were two mayors of Ottawa named Scott. The first was the first mayor of Bytown, John Scott, a lawyer. He served in 1847 and again in 1850. Richard William Scott was the second, also a lawyer, and he was mayor in 1852. Richard went on to be a high-up federal politician, married a professional singer and lived on Daly Avenue. Which Scott is the street named after, our first mayor or the more prominent one? Unknown.

The world is grey-white under a grey-white dome, and the bright orange famous pizza house stands out against the swirling air. When it was on Richmond until two years ago, the Newport was the centre of the Ottawa chapter of the Elvis Sighting Society. Hopefully Elvis has been made aware of the new location.

A path on the north side parallels the dry canal in which the Transitway runs, ferrying those Ottawans who chose to eschew the car as a commuter conveyance and reduce our collective carbon emissions. On the far side of the rapid bus route is Westboro Beach, and indeed there was once a path down to the river, along Roosevelt. On the south side of Scott, a vacant lot awaits a standard issue office block and, a little further east, the car park of the Granite Curling Club is almost full. The Granite, the youngest of the city clubs, opened for ends 61 years ago this month. It takes its name from its preferred stone. Until they used granite, irons were the standard, an iron being made of wood with a metal core. As I pass the club, a cyclist passes me, dressed for arctic skiing, the wheels of his bike fat as an old Model-T tire. He or she is passing the crawling cars.

Averting my eyes from the two stores a block apart selling hot tubs and spas (sigh) and cruelly reminding myself that somebody somewhere is having sun tan oil rubbed on their back, I turn down Lanark, cross the ugly transitway bridge to discover the entrance to the slender Metropole condo tower, which rises above Westboro Beach and is crowned by a glass-sided hat box of some sort. (It's a giant M, I now realize.) It's the only high rise in the beach area, and is visible from miles away, due to the fact that it is the second-highest building in the city. (Place de Ville is the highest.) A decade old, it is almost, almost, elegant and worth repeating, if giant condos we must have, elsewhere in the city, both for its solitude, and its attempt—forced on it by the locals—to limit its view blocking.

The International Buddhist Progress Society of Ottawa and a large log-walled retail store dedicated to outdoor pursuits sit next to each other on the south side; the inner and the outer side by side, yin and yang. On the other side of the street, in the dystopian, soulless concrete transitway Westboro Station, several smokers are in out of the wind, zenning themselves as they wait for the bus to arrive.

By the time I reach Island Park, the homebound traffic is gridlocked, the traffic lights playing commuter catch and release with the cars, all of them blowing off unhealthy steam from their sphincters. Looking up, I see the minaret of the Ottawa Mosque in the distance, while the tops of the cranes engaged in building a new condo to my right, mercantile minarets, are invisible. Looking back, my footsteps are already filled in with snow.

For some reason, the grey squirrels have chosen just one large maple in the backyard of a tidy postwar home on busy Scott Street to build multiple nests. While the winter-born young grow inside, the grey world below goes about its business, and I continue eastward. At the corner of Scott and Sir Frederick Banting (the insulin associated Nobel prize winner born in Ontario: came in fourth on the Greatest Canadians list; promises to do better next time), Tunney's Pasture begins, taking up 50 hectares between Scott and the River Parkway.

The Tunney in Tunney's Pasture was a farmer called Anthony, an Irishman who immigrated to Ottawa in the year of Confederation, build a home on Parkdale, and grazed cattle on the field beside him, with permission from a Lumbermen's Association who owned the pasture. In the middle of the 20th century, the lumbermen sold it to the government for the building of a campus dedicated to public service. Many of the original yellow brick buildings remain, but their simple grace has been overshadowed by the several Mussolini-esque gray towers on the campus that went up in the 70s. I worked in one of these, writing for the Canada Year Book, which was axed in 2012. The best part of the day was walking up to Wellington at lunchtime.

The main entrance to the Pasture is at Holland. The Holland family that gave their name to the north-south arterial road was an interesting bunch, founding members of the Ottawa Land Association. Two of the Hollands, brothers Andrew and George, were entrepreneurs anxious to introduce new technologies to Ottawa, including the phonograph and the Vitascope, which they displayed for the first time in Canada in West End Park, where Fisher Park School is now.

A small stretch of car-related, pleasantly untidy buildings starts up after Holland on the south side, and in the window of one repair shop a sign hangs with *Power is Nothing Without Control*. At first I think it has something to do with the present government, but it turns out to be a slogan designed to sell tires.

To complement the minaret of the Ottawa Mosque further west, the golden onion domes of the Russian Orthodox Church shine on the north side of the transitway. Is there a connection between centres of spiritual gathering and interesting architecture? Each branch of the tree of religions seems to find an eye-catching way to point heavenwards. Certainly the religious centres across the city are becoming the bastions of non-grayness, while the towers of commerce have nothing to say.

And here, a little way after Parkdale, which forms the boundary of Tunney's Pasture and is lined by a wall of condos north of Scott, is the boarded up, abandoned Odawa Native Friendship Centre, formerly a school built in 1933. Snow has piled up the steps all the way to the front door, and the silence within reverberates. As recently as 2012, the centre was commenting on the presence of a rogue elk on Scott, calling it a good omen for Ottawa, but the police shot the elk, and the Odawa closed, moving to the City

Centre. There is, surprise surprise, an unfriendly argument going on between the city and a developer as to how tall the condos that will replace the centre should be.

Now the road reaches Bayswater and it rises in a bridge over the railway lines, and on the south side the recently renovated, architectural oddity, the City Centre. I can hear the noise of construction as I walk up the bridge, and at the crest the worksite of the digging of the Confederation Line is full of workers dressed to beat the endless cold snap.

The stroll down Scott Street ends when I reach the point where it shape-shifts into Albert. Albert, named for a member of the British aristocracy by marriage, used to commence just before Booth heading east, but about a decade ago it was extended to reach the O-Train/Transitway intersection at Bayview.

Across from the swirl of Bayview, the curve of the architectural curiosity the City Centre dominates the skyline. Once a not-sure-what-to-do-with-itself kind of place, it has been re-clad in not-grey (my favourite colour) and is attracting brewers and bakers and perhaps soon a candlestick maker. Across the street from the centre is the once-upon-a-time depot for the street cars, now a more static self-storage.

Watching construction workers working is a favourite pastime in any city, and there is plenty to peruse in Ottawa lately.

The site devoted to the western portion of the tunnel that will house the Confederation line is a montage of hard hats, piles of rebar, and twin towers that look like oil patch machinery that I can see shaking. Mounting a snow-bank, the machinery reveals itself as a giant auger, the kind you would employ if you were ice fishing for whales. A pink cement truck alongside is waiting to dispatch its load into the earth.

Between Preston and Booth, the latter confusingly closed across the Flats during construction, it is possible to turn your head right and catch a glimpse of how LeBreton Flats might have looked if it had not been demolished in the mid-1960s. Particularly so on lower Lorne Avenue. The rear, natural wall of these streets is Nanny Goat Hill, a name people love to say and that reflects the goats that once flourished there under the eyes of the self-sustaining Dominican friars.

As Yogi Berra said, if you come to a fork in the road—take it, and by the bunkerish but benign yellow Good Companions (always liked that name) which is celebrating sixty years of gathering, Albert rises slowly to cross Bronson. Then it enters the ramparts of Ottawa's western downtown edge, as a one-way cross-towner heading west. Meanwhile the parallel strip of Slater is the route cars must take to access the business district. This little part of Ottawa up on a limestone plateau was known as Ashburham Hill. There's a town of Ashburham in Sussex, England. The first Queen Anne style house on the block, south-side, is the former home of a railway engineer built in 1864, the year Macdonald and Cartier were getting together a government, and hoping to have an airport named after them.

Walking past the Ottawa Technical School building an engraving in one of the façade stones reads: *This Stone Was Laid by His Excellency Lord Tweedsmuir Governor-General of Canada, 26th Day of May, 1939.* (His Lordship was the author John Buchan, and he wrote a novel set in Canada while in Rideau Hall, entitled *Sick Heart River.*) Originally there was a ladies college on the site, and the Tech moved there in the middle of World War I, and it got a Deco-ish expansion in Tweedsmuir's day. The school, which taught the trades and turned out several fine orchestral musicians, was at its peak in the Fifties, and is still in the guiding hands of the School Board.

Sidelining myself in the foyer of a hotel, I reset my thermostat and observe the visitors to Ottawa arriving and departing. Without fail the arrivals are greeted by hosts with the oh-so Ottawa salutations, "Sorry about the weather" or "Cold, enough for ya?" Me too, and yes, I silently reply and I'm back into it for the final stretch to Elgin.

Down here on the Albert Street sidewalk, the vaulting of the temperature to above zero for the first time in two months has energized the pedestrians. The mood of the street is one of release from a cold clutch; even the pools of people waiting at the string of bus stops ahead of me seem to be listening to happy tunes in their ear pods.

The downtown cross-streets—Queen, Albert, Slater, Laurier—are canyons now, their walls rising ever higher as older, shorter buildings of brick and stone cladding have been erased and a new skyline drawn, leaving a narrow scarf of sky overhead and a million windows, the workplaces of the sky-people. They awake in their condos above ground, briefly ride at street level and then rise up to their offices, thus spending most of their week above ground.

The massive black, cut-out walls of the Constitution Square triptych of buildings, with its impressive granite-clad portal displaying the only curve in the entire structure, dominates an entire block. In the small square across the road, the ice in the fountain has melted and some brave birds are wing washing. There are some curious objects in this square found almost nowhere else on the street, random in shape and moving slightly in the breeze. I think they are called trees.

Relief in scale and decoration appears on the southeast corner of Bank. Once the headquarters of Ottawa Hydro, the Art Deco gem there now houses a fair-minded local coffee shop. Next door, the advertisement painted on the side walls still attracts diners to the Cathay Chop Suey House, a veteran restaurant that I believe I ate in as a boy, almost sixty years ago, but is now closed and replaced by a louder dining establishment.

The stretch down to Metcalfe on the south side comprises mostly hotels of various star ratings, among them the former Beacon Arms. A fire in the "Broken" Arms fifty years ago killed three people including the mother of one of the firemen who fought it, and who was the switchboard operator who warned everyone to evacuate. Elvis rested up here before doing two shows at the old Auditorium on April 3rd, 1957. Downstairs was a music and comedy room, where I remember seeing hommie star comedian Mike McDonald do a homecoming set that left me fighting for breath.

The World Sexchange (Exchange) Plaza, as it is delightfully misnamed by the more playful Ottawans, opens out on the north side like a niche in the canyon walls. One or two coffee drinkers are standing in the sunshine that has deked through the skyline, and in a few short months there will be al fresco music playing here.

The Fuller Building at 75 Albert, close to Elgin on the north side, is actually starting to look vintage. A simple repeating pattern of white and black in the façade almost seems quaint. Built in 1960, it suffered an injurious collapse while under construction, and later a fire broke out on the roof. But it has been quiet for fifty-five years, and continues to wear the name of one of Ottawa's architectural and construction dynasties, founded by Thomas Fuller who was the Dominion Chief Architect in the late 19th century and the man who designed the first set of parliament buildings.

Opposite the Fuller is another sky-eating, glass-walled monolith, albeit in beige and light blue, a new government finance building replacing the old National Gallery and named for James Flaherty, the former finance minister. As I pause at Elgin to close my notebook, I notice several small sandwich boards placed on the sidewalk outside the building warning of the dangers of falling ice. Into every Ottawa street, some ice must fall.

Somerset Street West

Somerset at Arthur in the late 1920s.
Ottawa Boys' Club mid-left in the old firehall.

nce Ottawa really got going, there was money to be made in setting up and servicing the swelling work force, both bureaucratic and brawny. So it was the merchants that made the second-tier fortunes. The lumber barons had the biggest treasure chests, but the storeowners had cash in their coffers too. And then, as now, they put it into real estate.

Much of that merchant money went into homes in Centretown, residences like those that line the eastern end of Somerset West, near the Canal. In the last quarter of the 19th century this part of the street, all the way down to Bank, was like a twin line of dancers facing each other in their Sunday architectural best, the tree branches arching over; the way all streets should be. Of a morning it is not hard to visualize the doors opening and well-suited men taking to their carriages or walking in their fine leather shoes to work.

With my back to the ever-busy Corktown pedestrian bridge and the Ottawa U campus, I start out along the slight curve that takes Somerset West away from the Canal and points in a bee line towards Chinatown and on till it merges into Wellington. (Hurrah again for the Corktown Bridge. A grass roots request, at first resisted—cost too much—and finally started and finished. A rare success story.)

The splendid house on the northern corner, once the B and B of a well known, retired regional politician, turns out to be the Palestinian General Delegation. As is the habit in capital cities, several more splendid homes have been co-opted as Embassies and such on this couple of blocks. The nearby Syrian Embassy is in the former home (built in 1901) of the merchant Newell Bate. The very polite small gentleman, who asked me quite what I was doing as I squinted at the plaque by the Bate front door, chuckled as I gave him my flimsy credentials; probably the best story he'd heard that day. There is a pleasant, Canadian sort of irony to the fact that on this tranquil, Spring-is-coming day on the street reside the foreign delegations of two of the world's more troubled regions.

I detect an air of Scottishness in the design and naming of several dwellings as I cross Cartier and proceed towards Elgin.

Low-rise apartment blocks from the Thirties named *The McCormack* and such are a giveaway, and one house, to prove that every home is a castle to its owner, has a turret that is starting to lean. The Leaning Turret of Somerset. I pass the Adams House, built in 1888 by, according to its plaque, Sarah and Samuel Adams as an investment property. I note the wife's name coming first, and presumably Sam was not the American of the same name that brewed beer. One or two of the houses have art pieces in their small front gardens: a metal mobile and a simple thing of rock and steel rising at an angle.

The shade grows more engulfing as the mundane, taller apartment blocks appear, most of them wisely holding on to brick as the facing of choice. Outside one of them, a retired gentleman, the guardian of its shrubbery, is cleaning out the dead leaves from under a juniper bush. He pauses to light a cigar, takes a puff, and wishes a passerby a good afternoon.

St. Theresa's Church on the north side, dated 1929 and dedicated to a saint who had only been canonized four years earlier, is very bricky indeed, a sombre church with no signs of activity. Its website says that it was Deco-ishly designed by W. E. Noffke. I thought I knew all Noffke's buildings, but here is another.

The finest house on the row catches my eye, and its plaque states that both Gordon Pattee and Archibald Freiman lived here. Pattee was a lumber baron and, lucky for him, partner to William Goodhue Perley, who ran one of the biggest outfits in town in timber's heyday. Freiman, who arrived here from Lithuania in 1880, had a well-remembered department store on Rideau, where the Bay presently does the same thing. Now the old place is an Army Officers' Mess; hence the Canadian flag flying aloft.

And then, crossing O'Connor, the banners on ye olde lamp posts tell me I am in Somerset Village. A genuine effort, largely driven by the gay community, has made this block leading up to Bank one of the most attractive in the city, with many restaurants on the ground floor of the finely-maintained homes, human-rights organizations and the like above.

The find of the block has a gaudy plaque announcing that Mr. William Lyon Mackenzie King lived at this address in the first decade of the 20th century. He had quite a time of it while living here. In 1901 his roommate and buddy, Henry Harper, drowned trying to save a woman who had fallen through the ice at a skating party. (In honour of his friend, King gave money for the statue of gallant Sir Galahad on Parliament Hill.) He won a 1908 by-election, and got re-elected as our first Minister of Labour the year after. Twelve years later he was Prime Minister. (Actually, it seems this is not exactly King's house; that burnt down in 1997 and was lovingly replicated.)

Somerset Village stands proud until I reach the corner with Bank, where sits the derelict Duke of Somerset inn, part of which collapsed in 2007. The building, which started life in 1899 as a dry goods store, was undergoing renovations at the time. There's a shoebox pizzeria opposite the Duke, or what's left of him, after a ghastly entrance to a car park. On the car park exterior wall the enlightened proprietor has allowed a student at the School of Art to put up a colourful display of her work.

On the other side of Somerset Street across Bank, the south side, just past the bank turned restaurant with live music, turned supermarket, is where the Somerset Film Theatre used to be. I'm afraid to add up how many hours I spent in that wonderful cave, but they were all pleasant, as they are for any movie addict. And I recall once, before the movie started, an announcer came on to inform us that anyone talking loudly during the movie would be "taken outside and shot." Those were the days.

The couple of blocks between Bank and Lyon that I'm traversing now start out with a characterless but vital subsidized high rise, which has a clinic, an alterations shop and a community police station at the bottom. (Is there an architect in town who could design more attractive and enjoyable low-income and subsidized housing units? The punishment for being poor shouldn't include living in an Ugly.) It faces one of the city's better in-fills, a small cluster of town houses with shrubbery and an inner courtyard. Thereafter there are houses that were originally similar to those in the Somerset Village on the east side of Bank that have undergone serious cosmetic surgery, but here they have, for the most part, been allowed to show their age, and indeed one or two of them, unless rescued, may be destined for the old homes' home. And a few more trees wouldn't go amiss.

Dundonald Park, which occupies the block between Lyon and Bay, provides its neighbours with a permanent opportunity to get recreational or practice Tai-Chi, as well as a place named after an earl on a street named after a duke. On this windy mid-afternoon in the park there are several kids wearing themselves out on the oh-so-safe ugly plastic play structures, and two men transporting a twenty-four box of beer each on their shoulders away from the beer store, the hoser equivalent of women carrying laundry bundles back from the river. The more little parks like Dundonald across the city, the merrier we all will be.

Side by side in the park are two angled plaques, one federal in origin and the other municipal, commemorating the same event. The plaques are the result of the efforts of local historian Andrew Kavchak, and looking up from the plaques at the Forties streamline brick apartment block opposite, with its little round windows, I am staring back in history to what some have called the very start of the Cold War, right here in Ottawa. The events that emanated from this building in 1945, set in motion by Mr. Gouzenko, a Soviet defector, make an appealing, exciting story. Yours to discover if you haven't already.

The blue street sign on the northwest corner of the park carries the word "Somerset" in Chinese below the English, and this signals that Chinatown starts here, at the intersection with Bay. Every Canadian city worth its dim sum has a clustered Chinese, make that Asian, community within itself that feeds its own and most of the rest of the city in an almost unbroken chain of restaurants and Chinese calligraphy. It would take, I'm sure, half a year to eat in them all at a rate of one a night, and the family tables seem bigger here than elsewhere in the city. And at least one of those nights must be spent witnessing the karaoke phenomenon that is China Doll, the singing drag queen stroke chef who belts them out on Fridays and Saturdays; catch him doing Etta James' *At Last* and your eardrums will never be the same again. And you can dress up too, as many do.

The shop windows hereabouts are full of miniature Buddhas and fountains and plastic toys with flappy ears and other cultural artifacts that a tourist would call trinkets, and the general ambiance (which somebody once told me is French for "dimmer switch') seems so much busier than on any other city street.

Chinatown is a still-growing place, spreading out squid-like as fast as the real estate will allow. I recall coming here as a brat with my parents, when perhaps there was only a handful of restaurants, but the Shanghai claims to be the first, a converted grocery store that started serving meals in a bowl in 1971, so perhaps that's a false memory. The area got an Asian injection in the early-'80s with Project 4000, the Boat People infusion, steered to success by Ottawa's best mayor to date, Marion Dewar. It was officially labelled Chinatown only in 2005 (it had previously been Somerset Heights) many years after the rest of the city had started calling it that.

This stretch of Somerset is also, I'm happy to say, enjoying a revival of '60s coffee houses with a Wi-Fi twist. You know the sort of place—mismatched furniture and crockery, a couch or two, very relaxed atmosphere, local art on the walls, healthy menu leaning towards organic and fair trade and such, and quite right too. I find them far preferable to the generic, franchised non-local American chains, and much easier to pass the time in.

Crossing over Bronson, which is easy to do on the south side as the street is blocked to traffic while they tear it up, I notice the former site of the La Roma, with its distinctive red and white tile work, is a take-out pizza joint.

Then the Arch looms up in all its glory. Similar to the one at the entrance to Chinatown in Montreal, this one known as a Paifang in Mandarin, is part in-your-face propaganda, part ethnic-symbolic statement, part public art. Chinatown began raising money for it twenty years ago, and it came to pass in October 2010. I like it for its eccentricity if not its beauty, and it contrasts favourably with the Little Italy arch on Preston.

Rising from the uncomfortable bench by the new arch in Chinatown to resume my walk, I recall that this must have been the site of the Grads tavern, a hostelry of considerable rough repute in its day. It burnt down in January 1991, and moved down the street to the corner of Bayswater, where it was closed permanently by the police after a man was beaten to death outside it. (A video of local poet Michael Dennis reading an honest poem inside the old Grads during the Festival of the Arts in 1988 is available on the Net.)

A similar tavern further along at Rochester Street (named after a venerable Ottawa family that provided mayors and for a while an entire suburb, Rochesterville) was the Vendome. Local writer Brian Doyle, who lived around here, was there the night the Vendome burnt down, and he remembers witnessing the ladies who worked there in, um, "apparel removal" asking the firemen if they could retrieve their costumes.

No doubt it is simply coincidence, but as I am proceeding away from the gateway westwards and downhill through the heart of Chinatown a gentleman on the sidewalk in sunglasses is performing martial arts kata, or patterns. He is both good and oblivious of the stares he is drawing from the team of hard-hatted city workers opposite who are affecting major sidewalk and sewage pipe repair. (Perhaps rather than "heart" of Chinatown, I should substitute "liver," since it is within that organ that the oriental soul lies.)

The majority of the stores and businesses along here are devoted mainly to the stomach. The restaurants are cheek to cheek, and in between are well-stocked grocery stores, their entrances lined with opened cardboard produce boxes. Despite the street works the grocers have put their wares out on trestle tables as usual, the legs propped up with bits of wood to bring the tables level. What with the noise of backhoes and the multiplicity of signage on the street, the decibel level seems extraordinary. Two signage curiosities: a corner drug store has filled its windows with life-size photographs of happy smiling multi-cultural people, and yet there is not an Asian face among them. And the supermarket windows nearby are still wishing me a Merry Christmas.

Outside the Dalhousie Community Centre at 755 Somerset (which may be called the heart of the street) a woman in a large Senators' jersey is seated waiting for ParaTranspo. The Centre (the name "Dalhousie" refers to the fact that it is in the former Dalhousie Ward) is in what used to be the St-Jean Baptiste School, for this is the parish of the patron saint of the French-Canadians. As if on cue a young Dominican friar crosses my path on his way to his seminary home on the top of Nanny Goat Hill. It was the young Dominican's antecedents that gave the Hill its name. The original friars kept goats on their self-sustaining garden.

Half way between Bronson and Preston it is possible to pause on the corner of Empress and see a quartet of churches in a pleasant range of architectural styles; the Britishy St. Lukes, which was opened by Sir Robert Borden in 1922; the Sixties-looking Greek Orthodox Holy Trinity opposite; just off the street to the north the Chinese Christian church and to the south I can see the back of the Annunciation Orthodox. There must be quite a cacophony of praise hereabouts on a Sunday.

Strolling down towards the corner with Preston I note that work has still not begun on the Vietnamese Boat People museum. Perhaps there is a fund-raising issue. As I have noted before when I walked down Preston, this corner feels like a sort of Marco Polo crossroads, Italians to the north and south, Asians to the East and West, with a large tire garage puncturing the illusion.

The street renovations now are complete on the Somerset Street West Bridge, the one that goes over the O Train Line. After passing a wine-making store and a fairly new, vast antiques emporium, which of course I have to enter and circumnavigate, I stand at the high point waiting for a train to pass under me.

I can see the City Centre, of which I am fond architecturally as it is a fine balance of form and function, and directly below, at 290 City Centre Road, a much neglected single-story brick building in the Queen Anne style, rather like one of our early library branches. There is nothing else like it around, but it could be a little gem if cleaned up.

It is a short walk down the bridge to the end of Somerset, where it braids into Wellington at Somerset Square, which is a triangle. On the way I pass the second Indian restaurant on the street claiming to have the best butter chicken in town, an empty Dollarama store that has a city of Ottawa notice in its window claiming that application has been made by a developer to put up a *twenty-seven* story condo. The apartment block nearby at Bayswater, which seems plenty high enough to me, is fifteen stories. That's a lot of daylight getting taken up.

Incidentally, the innovative artist Justin Wonnacott who lives in the area and has contributed several fine works of public art to the city, has photographed many of the addresses I have been walking past. You can see them on his website. It's a colourful exhibit.

Sparks Street Mall

Postcard of the early days of the Sparks Street Mall.

*S*tanding at the east end of the Sparks Street Mall, with the War Memorial and Confusion Square at my back, I'm fishing in my memory for the day in 1961 when, as a ten-year old, I walked with my family along the then exciting experiment that the National Capital Commission was, well, test-walking—a pedestrian mall, a street unavailable to cars. This was two years after the glorious streetcars had ceased running down Sparks.

I see on my internal memory screen a sunny day and happy, strolling Ottawans in no hurry to get anywhere. They must have remained happy because, after trying the experiment several more times over the next five years, the NCC went ahead and made the Mall a permanent fixture of downtown Ottawa in 1966. It was mentioned in speeches several times on opening day that this was "North America's First Pedestrian Mall."

Looking now westward down the Mall on a mid-week winter's afternoon, I notice that one actually can't look westward down the Mall on any day. An informational, metal and concrete rotunda plus a very good life-size statue of a rearing bear block the view, as do several more rotundas down the length of the walkway all the way to Bank Street, artfully impeding the flow at each corner. Looking across the floor of the rotunda nearest me, which is dangerously iced up, I can see a welcoming poster and an index of shopping and dining opportunities listed alongside it. The index reveals there are five souvenir stores on the Mall and, apart from an up-market bar offering a lounge singer, not the slightest hint of any cultural goings on.

Irish music is tinkling out of small speakers from above the doorway of the D'Arcy McGee's pub on the southern corner at Elgin. There has pretty well always been a hostelry on this corner since Ottawa was a dirt road in the woods. A century or so ago, give or take a few years, one might have seen Wilfrid Laurier, Oscar Wilde and Anna Pavlova on the Sparks Street sidewalk outside the luxurious Russell Hotel, though not all at the same time. In fact, Sir Wilfrid lived in the hotel for ten years. And one night, at a dinner in the Russell, a certain Lord Stanley offered to stump up for a cup for the nation's top hockey team. The Russell (it was east of D'Arcy's; there were buildings on the other side of Elgin) was Ottawa's Chateau Laurier before the Chateau Laurier arrived in 1912 and the Russell lost its alpha male status. It sat abandoned for while and then, as abandoned building in Ottawa are wont to do, burnt down in 1927, at the age of sixty-two.

Some workers are installing brand new benches further along the mall from Darcy's, and the outdoor cafés that will eat up the centre of the Mall when the snow goes are not yet out, so strolling westward, forty-eight years after I did it as a boy, is pleasant; there is no threat of having to negotiate milling tourists. My history-hungry eye is drawn to the buildings that were here in my childhood and before that. Number 62, which is now a philatelist's, has an Art Deco front, Art Deco being the period in which I wish to be reborn, if one is allowed to be reborn backwards. The wonderful honey-coloured limestone that fronts the building above the black granite sheeting is the only example of this glorious stone left in the city. It sits next to the Ottawa Electric Building, which is where Ahearn and Soper, Ottawa's first utilities millionaires and streetcar owners, had their offices. Thomas Ahearn was born in Ottawa, in 1855, the year it graduated to a city.

The helpful gentleman inside number 62 explains that Kimmerley Stamps has been here only eighteen months, having fled a building from further along the street that was declining (and has since given up to the point of its roof collapsing, a warning sign about the general state of the Mall, and of which more later). The first occupant of this site, in 1869, was a jeweller, John Leslie. (The Leslie family home eventually became Laurier House, after Laurier moved out of the Russell.) Then it was an Imperial bank with a high ceiling; the ceiling and the bank manager's polished metal-framed office are still here, as is the vault, at the owner's insistence when Kimmerley moved in. That insistence, which is to be applauded, was also the reason the building sat empty for many a year.

On the other side of the Street is the Hope Building, named not after the human sentiment but the man who had it built in 1910, James Hope, bookseller. It was one of Ottawa's first high-ish rises, erected to the very tip of the height restriction put in place that year, an edict similar to the one in Paris that limits buildings to seven stories. The words "Bible House" at the top were added by a later occupant, when the Christian Science Monitor reading room was to be found within.

Back on the even-numbered side of the street, however, at number 90, is a building that stands out in its awfulness, like a belch in the midst of a chamber orchestra, like an ogre at the ballet. It is everything the Hope Building is not, and the hand of modern finance is detectable in the banal glass and steel and right-angles and complete lack of ornamentation. (Morgan's department store once stood here, a much more elegant edifice.) This is the Royal Bank Plaza, designated the Thomas D'Arcy McGee building by its shared occupants, the federal government. How it managed to bully its way onto the Mall is beyond me, but it is the ruination of it. The Mall has been mauled by it.

The touristy usefulness of Thomas D'Arcy McGee, Father of Confederation, haunts the Mall, since he was assassinated just a little bit further along the Mall on April 6th, 1868. He was shot as he returned from a late night session of Parliament. An orator with a love of language, McGee would have appreciated that buildings too have something to say, and that this building named after him is essentially mute, and if it could speak, it would be only to offer numbers and percentages.

My westward stroll takes me past the boarded up front of the E. R. Fisher store. The Fisher family enjoyed a presence on the Mall for over a century, but several factors, not least the arrival of governmental landlords on the north side of the Mall in the 1970s, and the hunt for parking that afflicts many potential Mall visitors, got behind them and pushed them into Westboro, a part of town where the attraction of low-level, diverse, street-retail is understood and cherished, at least for now.

Crossing Metcalfe I wish someone would hurry up and invent a new class of disabled-friendly pedestrian bridges, a device of which the Venetians have installed quite a few. I suddenly recall attending the Saturday morning movies at the Centre Cinema, by myself, at the age of ten. I would take the streetcar in from adolescent Elmvale Acres, my return fare clenched in one hand, and then walk to the cinema, paying with the money cocooned in the other hand. Once inside, I mostly remember watching men in masks running along the tops of trains or jumping onto horses

The Centre Cinema opened in 1915 at 110 Sparks next to Murphy-Gamble department store and just east of the home of the *Ottawa Citizen*, when the paper had a downtown presence. So, the Mall has a cultural, as well as an architectural and shopping history. Well before my time, Bennett's Vaudeville Theatre on the Mall, in 1907, was the first venue in the city to commence regularly showing moving pictures. The Regent, which was down at the corner of Bank, opened in 1916, and it was the first picture house in town where films with sound were heard in Ottawa, and only closed in the 1970s. Thus I remember the Mall not for its mercantile drawing power but as a cultural venue, a place that catered to the mind in equal measure to other appetites.

The Mall still boasts architectural curiosities and fineries that grace the eye, and it is well to digest as much beauty as you can walking the streets of Ottawa, before it is all replaced by banality. Looking up, I catch the row of sculpted faces on the old Merchant's Bank, built in 1870, that depict the bank's first board of trustees, most of who appear to be registering shock at the present state of capitalism. Are we, I wonder, at the stage yet when the new can be employed to explain the old, and touch screens embedded in walls can explain the anecdotal history of the building in which they are housed; Touch, and you learn who Nicholas Sparks was, and in which year he laid out the street (1848). Poke, and you discover that this, the Bate Building, is the oldest standing structure on the strip, built for a grocery king in 1859.

The point I am strolling towards here, as I'm sure you have already divined, is that the Mall, as long as it is dedicated pretty much solely to the extraction of money from those who venture onto it, is doomed. A visitor from the Lake District of England I met remarked that there were far more concrete flower boxes, in what were apparently tank traps left over from World War Two, than trees, and that she would not have been surprised to find a sentry post at each end of the Mall, manned by someone demanding to know if you have any money left, and if so, why are you leaving?

Disheartening as it is by day in three of our seasons, it is a sadder place after the sun goes down; the spirit of the street goes down with it. Yes, the NCC claims to be revitalizing their side of the street, the south, bit by bit. They are including residential units (or "homes" as they are sometimes known) and retail outlets but there is no mention in the plans for somewhere for culture vultures to go, for night life.

An example, the back of the CBC building (CBC stands for Constantly Being Cut) which offers only dark windows onto the Mall, could do worse than provide Sparks with a small CBC museum and shop. Ottawa could finally solve its jazz-club problem with a Parisian or Liverpudlian style cellar club. Yes, there is a lounge bar, *Jazz'oo's*, with a touch of the Ritz, but otherwise live night music has largely fled the Mall. And could there at least be something called the Ottawa Shop, where a selection of the artistic output of the city could be available for purchase by tourists? Sparks was the first Ottawa street to be paved with asphalt, in 1895; it became North America's first pedestrian mall seventy years later. Are there some fresh cultural firsts in the Mall's future or is it destined to gradually decline as a gathering place, to grow stale? And to stay quiet at night?

St. Laurent Boulevard

St. Laurent Boulevard.

*I*t is a perfect day for a walk. It is as though autumn has gone into temporary remission and given us a slice of the summer we never really had, but the streets are more colourful than summer with the leaves turned the tricolor of traffic lights beneath a cloudless sky. Perfect enough even for a walk down St. Laurent Boulevard.

Every North American, car-stuffed city has a St. Laurent Boulevard, an arterial road mostly devoted to servicing those in search of the perfectly outfitted life within their income level (and beyond) and a matching car. Edward Burtynsky had a stunning shot in his recent exhibition devoted to our relationship to oil at the Natural History Museum; it depicts a long, long street in modern Anywhereville devoted to commercialism, a parade of wallet-seducing, high-flying signs and static cars in rows. It instantly reminded me of St. Laurent.

St. Laurent Boulevard is named after our twelfth prime minister and is pronounced without difficulty in the French manner by Ottawans, although I once heard an American tourist rhyme it with torrent. It is a sandwich: the thick smoked meat of commercialism in the middle with residential white bread either end. I start at the northern end, outside the gates of the RCMP and Police College campus. I take one step forward down the boulevard, and then several back, realizing I have not been on the campus since I learnt to swim there aged three. There is no security post to pass through, but then the whole place is one big security post, if I think about it.

A small, recent pile of road apples at the side of a building testify that it is the arena, built in 1939 with an Art Deco entrance, of the Musical Ride. I walk inside to stand a moment in the primal smell of manure and sawdust. There is, a sign says, to be a horse auction here at the weekend; I hadn't realized the horses were for sale when their show biz careers were over. A quick tour of the rest of the campus shows it to be mostly of pleasant brick buildings, rather like a Bostonian university. Several sweaty trainee officers run past me getting in a lunchtime jog.

Heading south and stepping aside for three immaculate black cars with tinted windows coming out of the RCMP gates, I spy several older men with brooms on the tree-lined sidewalks returning homeward; not a leaf clearing patrol but curlers après their game. The homes are small here, but beautifully groomed as though they have collectively entered a competition for best-kept section of the boulevard.

I'm passing into the older section of the Manor Park neighbourhood, which stands on former marshy ground that was once crisscrossed with riding trails. In the late 1940s several developers got together and created a grid of homes on the filled-in marsh for families of modest incomes, including several quadrangles of single-storey, conjoined town houses of red brick with slight Georgian touches about the doors.

It was into one of these quadrangles that Father, Mother and I moved in 1952, as did many other starter families newly recruited for the National Research Centre. As I walk through one of the inner square paved courtyards no memories come to me, but I do recall my mother later referring to them as "the barracks" and complaining of nowhere for kids to play. We lasted three years. A gentleman cleaning his older model car says hello to me in an Asian accent and remarks on the quality of the day.

The southern boundary of Manor Park is the Beechwood Cemetery, into which I turn right through a modest gate for a brief commune with my neighbours in time. Just past the sign that announces this as the National Military cemetery, a Chinese pagoda sits atop a mound, ringed by small fruit trees and flanked by an empty hedged park of tranquility. On the far side of the pagoda a plaque on a post informs me that, before it was devoted to the deceased, this ground was a hundred acre farm belonging to the McPhails. Mr. McPhail worked on the building of the Rideau Canal. He sold the farm to the cemetery developers in 1873, and a McPhail, Annie, lived within the grounds until the 1920s. There is a film somewhere in there about that family saga.

Back on St. Laurent, after a couple of restaurants have appeared opposite the cemetery, the strip malls commence. The first has cunningly included the word Rockcliffe in its title and indeed there is a yoga studio and an epicurean deli transferred here after a fire on Beechwood a couple of years ago. In the adjacent mall to the south there is a canine school (teaching the three Rs; running, writhing and reacting loudly) and a man in tails smoking a cigarette outside a funeral co-operative. He appears to be showing me how to hasten the day when I'll need his services. A couple of churches and a small, lower-power substation separate the Protestants from the Catholics and then I have Notre-Dame Cemetery on my right shoulder. It is more densely inhabited and less finely landscaped, the final resting place of over one hundred thousand people and counting. It opened the year before the McPhails sold their farm. A wall of boxy highrise apartments known collectively as the Highlands on a bit of a hill sit opposite Notre-Dame. They are still among the highest buildings in the city, and the roof top view must go all the way to the tree line. And now I'm at Montreal Road and the car dealerships have started.

As I'm walking down St. Laurent from Montreal Road to Industrial I realize the reason for the slightly uneasy feeling that is dogging me. I am *walking*. I am, in a sense, a visible minority, in that there are very few other walkers or cyclists; rather there is an endless, noisy parade of vehicles. I feel as though I am being studied, if I am noticed at all by the drivers, as a visible curiosity. A biped that had escaped from a more walkable neighbourhood. For the most part the only other bipeds I see are getting in and out of their cars in the slots provided in front of strip malls of varying size and complexity.

A brief stretch of modest single-dwelling houses ensues, all of which, I hope, are blessed with triple glazing. I imagine the inhabitants all wandering round wearing noise-elimination headphones, communicating using sign language or writing short sentences on tablets. Surely here is a need for as many trees as could be crammed in. With their ability to absorb noise, like windbreaks in large farmed fields, and look good, they would do the street a big favour. In amongst the more modest homes, in the 700 block, is an older, porched brick house, it too a visible minority in its throwback style. I have noticed these anachronistic domiciles all over Ottawa, homes that have somehow kept their heads while all around are losing theirs. They are like a scattered tribe of Homies.

Now I do spot a clump of people, young men in the school field between Queen Elizabeth and Rideau High. They seem underdressed for football, and then I realize they are playing rugby. I stand for a moment and receive a montage of memories from my time on the school rugby field, which usually ended with me exiting early, blood pouring from my glass nose. (Later, back home, I go on the two schools' respective websites. They have slogans like *Educating for Success!* under their names now, and seem to be competing with each other, as though they were businesses. Queen Elizabeth has a whole page about how to deal with young people and their cell phones, the primary source of their attention, and the amount of advertising daily they will be subjected to, fledgling consumers that they are.)

As I proceed I begin to read the street rather than observe it. I feel I am drowning in the sheer quantity of words plastered everywhere on stores, store windows, on billboards standing on poles anywhere there is a tiny patch of open ground or old railway line overgrown by scrub. Almost all of it is written in the language of enticement, and so anything that isn't in that vein stands out. My eye catches the words Canada Council for the Arts, and I remember that the Art Bank HQ is here. They have just had an open day at the end of the previous month. The Art Bank was founded in 1972—the woman who started it, Suzanne Rivard Le Moyne, died a year ago—and it is a civilized brokerage of tax dollars.

Once I reach Donald and carry on south, the gloves come off, and the arterial roadway gives up all pretense of being part of a neighbourhood and is a barely broken row on either side of commercialism. A relentless signage war is underway to get my attention, and they all seem to be shouting, the loudest noise coming from one of those stores that offers expensive money loans to people who don't have much of it. The side streets now only serve to separate the strip malls, and it is all about cars. Car lots. Tire stores. Auto repair stores. Car stereos. Windscreens. Discounts. Prices ending in .99.

Once past St. Laurent Shopping Centre (in the car park of which I learnt to do doughnuts; a rite of winter driving for the sons and daughters of nearby neighbourhoods) and under the

Queensway—the traffic is, of course, crawling at about 90k under its speed limit—the signage goes up in the air. To my right the letters spelling out OC Transpo hang high above me, with the stables holding the buses below, red fronts poking out of each garage like race horses on wheels. To my left the sloping letters CUPE (Canadian Union of Public Employees) are aloft. No doubt the building is abroil with equal quantities of foreboding and forlorn hope; it is the day of the throne speech.

After walking over two bridges with old, overgrown railway yard underneath, another "parking" opportunity, meaning not a car-park but a park park— the traffic next to me is crawling towards a gleefully sadistic set of lights at Industrial, and I figure I've sucked in my daily dose of greenhouse gases, and take a tea break. There has been, as I have written about recently, a groundswell of desire for the rehabilitation of our streets under the banner of Complete Streets. The policy got the verbal (so far) endorsement of the City in the transportation master plan. It may be too late for St. Laurent Boulevard to re-boulevard it, but it could proudly serve as an example not be repeated.

After trekking the middle section of St. Laurent Boulevard, a stretch of street that seems to be constantly shouting at you, I step into an art gallery in a low-browed strip-mall on the east side, intrigued by the very restful, uncluttered landscapes in the window, and find myself in what the man behind the desk claims is the biggest commercial gallery in Ottawa. I pass a peaceful ten minutes or so in a subjective frame of mind. The place is empty except for me, it being late afternoon. The fast food bordello next door is full.

A few steps further along on the same side of the road, and I'm walking on grass. Sharing the parkland I've entered are a lighthouse, a shiny stainless-steel rocket and a grand steam train engine. This is because deeper eastward, at the rear of the parkland, sits the Canadian Science and Technology Museum, housed in a former bakery warehouse.

Crossing the boulevard to the west side, I pass a reflective moment in Alda Burt Park, a compact bit of green with a wading pool and a magnificent willow tree. Formerly known plainly as St. Laurent Park, it was renamed in 1986 after one of the founding families of Elmvale Acres (the others being the Dempseys and the Bradley-Coles). Mrs. Alda Burt, then ninety-two, opened the park that bears her name.

The temptation is to assume that St. Laurent continues directly southward at the Smyth Road intersection, but it fact it dekes right and then straightens out and heads for Walkley, first passing the Elmvale Acres Shopping Centre. There are signs stuck in the grass framing the car park advertising flu shots in the local drug store. The centre itself contains a library branch and a beer store next to each other, an interesting piece of juxtaposition that I doubt is repeated elsewhere in the city. The library window features books on diabetes and the upcoming Remembrance Day. Before the shopping centre was built, the local candy store for the kids escaping their brand new homes in the Acres was Tom Dempsey's. Let me here confess that I once stole a chocolate bar from Dempsey's on a dare, in 1958.

St. Laurent Boulevard resumes its residential role for the next few blocks, a scattering of high-rises towering over the shopping centre then the single dwelling houses, some side-on with carports, of Elmvale Gardens and Hawthorne Park. On one corner a fountain stands in a patch of green, a neighbourly touch, testament to the collective need to decorate architectural plainness and repetition. The presence of Hawthorne Public School on the west side is a reminder that beneath this stretch of St. Laurent lies a dirt track that once carried horse-drawn carriages into and out of the village of Hawthorne.

The condensed version of the story of Hawthorne goes something like this. All the way back in the 1830s, a gentleman named Green, a sawmill owner, initiated a small settlement near the present junctions of Walkley, Russell and St. Laurent. Hawthorne Road runs south of Walkley from this junction. Others who moved in came to call it Green's Corners and they put up a log schoolhouse in 1859. The hamlet retained the name Green's Corners until 1873, when the postmaster, for some reasons, changed the settlement's name to Hawthorne. By that time a replacement, bigger wooden school had been built near the first one, and then in 1899 Hawthorne got a redbrick one-roomer, which lasted until the school I just walked past was built in 1961. Meanwhile, Ottawa had absorbed Hawthorne village in the 1950s, which means there are old folks in town who were once card-carrying Hawthorne residents.

After surviving the crossing of Walkley to the south side, I look eastward towards the distant highway and can imagine Green's Corners sitting there, although I am no doubt superimposing a movie set, log homes and smoke curling from chimneys, schoolchildren filing through snow. The Boulevard arrows down, and makes a gentle curve westwards now and thereafter snakes through the St. Laurent Business Park. The first building on the west side is walled, anonymous and has a heavy security gate. There are government border services buildings nearby, so perhaps they are linked in some way. There seems to be a hushed air about the street now. I feel like there is a camera somewhere trained on me.

The park is a mix of high-techery, firms who want to manage my money and help me make more without working for it, an Islamic Centre and a nearby parking lot full of army vehicles at the back of an armoury. Everyone indoors seems to be going about their business very quietly, thinking hard, doing meetings or just clock watching. By the time I reach the absolute southwestern end of St. Laurent Boulevard where it Ts with Don Reid Drive, I am ready for the warmth of home and a woodstove.

St. Patrick Street

1920s view of St. Patrick looking east from Sussex.

*F*rom the moment many hundreds of Irishmen turned up to sweat out the making of the canal, there was going to be a St. Patrick Street in Ottawa. A street surveyor, working on a nice flat slab of land with water on three sides that was to become Lowertown, laid St. Patrick out in 1836 and it ran between two rivers, the Ottawa and the Rideau, a steamboat dock and inn at the Ottawa end and a wharf at the other. Gentlemen, start your horses and carts.

The street nowadays runs between two bridges—the cantilevered Alexandria, and the well-named St. Patrick Street Bridge that decants divisions of motorists into New Edinburgh. I start out to cover the street with my back to the Alexandra Bridge, and walk past Major's Hill Park to my right, Nepean Point and the tundra garden and agora of the Art Gallery to my left. A man standing under the giant Lord of the Rings spider outside the gallery looks up, and appears to be calling the bronze statue of the radio operator on the Peacekeeping Monument. In the past, in that short distance, three of those places— the park, the agora and the point—used to have concerts. Now they do not, and the city is less joyous with their loss.

I catch the light at Sussex, cross by permission of the striding white man, and slip into the Beaux Arts Court on the southeast corner. The centrepiece here in this little gem is a raised, life-sized angel (if angels are indeed our size), one that lowers her eyes from the stern gaze of Bishop Guigues on his lesser pedestal on the other side of the street. The Angel previously stood on top of the mortuary chapel at Notre-Dame Cemetery, so her outlook has improved.

There now commences on the south side of St. Patrick a run of domestic architecture that can be matched against any in the city. Walking along it for a history buff like me is a treat; no two buildings alike, some tasty history morsels. The small, simple-white worker's cottage at the start at number 138 is named after the master carpenter who lived there, Pierre Rochon. Pierre did the wood carving in the stalls and sanctuary in the Basilica as it was being built, in around 1844. It feels like one could peek through the windows of Rochon house into the mid-nineteenth century; see the family à table, wood shavings on the floor. The house itself may well have been built the year the Rideau Canal opened, 1832. That's Ottawa old.

Next to Rochon House, a jump in time and income bracket. The handsome, stone building next door was built in 1866 as the office and residence of Dr. François-Xavier Valade. It boasts a very elegant cantilevered second-storey balcony, from which, if

I lived there, I could discretely watch the comings and goings in the old stone Archbishop's Palace across the street. Valade's claim to fame is that he was asked, in 1885, to decide on the sanity of Louis Riel just prior to his trial. The doctor's home includes a carriageway to the back, through which I glimpse a boy playing badminton with his dog, this on the day of the Olympic scandal in the same sport. I think the dog is winning.

On we go. A modest, classy late-19th-century duplex with a splendid Katsura tree in front, and beside that an ordinary art gallery two-storey redbrick made splendid with a much filigreed bright white combination porch/balcony/cornice to match. This magnificent facade is recent, reconstructed from photographs and involving over three hundred hand crafted pieces. Then here is a Forties three-floor brick, all straight lines with an add-on enclosed portico all the way up; next a genteel semi-colonial with a fine sculpture out front (I regard art works in front gardens as gifts from the owners to the passing public); another Forties apartment block without the portico and some nice bricking detail; a home with a Quebec City balcony that hopefully has been the scene of many a wasted afternoon; then a final flourish of two more homes, one with a Greek style pillared entrance and then a traditional French-Canadian dormered affair. Standing on the corner with Parent, looking back down this architectural carnival, I feel like applauding.

On the other side of the street, just outside the black railings of the parking lot at the back of the Basilica, a little concrete structure that looks like a road salt box or some such turns out to be the support for a commemorative plaque. It was on this spot that care for the city's homeless, Ottawa's medical health infrastructure and education for young Catholic women all started. This was courtesy of Sister Elisabeth Bruyère who arrived in 1845 in a coach with seven Grey Nun Sisters. She moved them into rented accommodation on this spot and opened a house of compassion, including almost immediately nursing the sick during a typhoid epidemic. Many citizens died but miraculously none of the nuns. Sister Elisabeth possessed one of the city's great hearts, and the nearby hospital, hospice and community clinics bear her name proudly.

Between Parent and Dalhousie, the domestic architecture festival is only just a tad less satisfying, with Brousseau Terrace on the south side and Barrett Lane on the north as the exemplary examples. The former has a double carriageway, and a cornice that didn't need to be that elaborate but is the better for it. The latter is one of the superior integrations of new building into a historic existing row in town that I know of. It sits next to a 1908 double and is seamless. And it all ends with a beauty salon with a sandwich board outside that wonders if passers by are "NOT SATISFIED WITH YOUR SILHOUETTE?" Not something I ask myself very often, but now that you come to mention it, who is?

It takes me a moment to work out the problem with the stretch of St. Patrick from Dalhousie to Cumberland. No trees. But as I make note of the succession of businesses I am passing I realize that in this one block is practically a small village. It includes a yoga parlour in an old house on the corner (once the campaign headquarters of Alex Munter when he ran for mayor. Oh well), a funeral home, a pizzeria that announces it's been around since 1985. Maybe pizza years are like dog years, and that makes it old. There's also a "traditional" barber shop, a dry cleaners that includes the ever-advancing word "Eco" in its name and, in a small converted house, an Ottawa institution, the publishing house of poet Jacques Flamand, Les Editions Vermilion. Flamand is a tireless player/manager/champion for French-Canadian literature in our city, and was appointed to the Order of Ontario in 2009.

At the end by Cumberland sits St. Brigid's, a church converted into an arts centre by the local Irish community and a small, under-stocked park on the north side, named after Raphael Brunet. Back in the mid-'80s, when the park was fenced in and bigger, it was a staging ground for hookers and druggies, and there was concern over their interaction with the kids from the nearby school. Now it's unfenced and, today at least, empty.

St. Brigid's, whose pair of High Victorian unmatched steeples are the highest structures on the block, is hosting Chamberfest concerts as I pass by and the scattered noise of a sound check is coming through the open door. It opened for service in 1890, as a spiritual locus, separate from the Basilica down the road, for the tribal Irish Catholics of Lowertown. The congregation put up a good fight when the decision was made to close the doors, basically because the repair bill had become too big, but they lost and it was deconsecrated in 2006. The architect, James R. Bowes, handled quite a few commissions for the diocese. He died in a boarding house fire in California two years after the church opened.

From Cumberland down to the constantly shape-shifting King Edward, there is a pleasant mélange of housing: some that have been smartened up, one finely so, some infill, and others prepared to just let entropy take its course. At the junction, where it is easy to lighten your load of pocket change into the hats and cups of the panhandlers, there is a standard issue coffee shop, from the chain that has studiously closed its eyes to the health revolution in fast food. Opposite that a garage with some limited car sales.

I make it across King Edward safely, and there is a character shift, with pockets of cooperative housing both sides and a curious oasis of five older houses on the corner with Forsey Street, which I had never been on before. It leads to Bordeleau Park, which is a real gem, a bonus for those Lowertown residents east of King Edward.

The impressive Chinese Embassy, one of our stock of ex-Catholic buildings, somehow radiates an isolationist vibe. Today, for once, there is not a Falan Gong protester performing slow tai-chi-like moves, or sitting very still beside a banner lent up against a fence. Usually there is at least one there, and has been for years, perhaps ever since the Chinese bought the place in 1972 from the Sisters of the Good Shepherd. The embassy staff with offices at the back must have a fine view of the Rideau River. On the other side of the street, on the playing fields of De La Salle École Secondaire, young women are playing soccer on the very day their national counterparts take a bronze medal in the Olympics.

As a place to retire or go into long-term care, there probably isn't a more salubrious site to do so than on Porter's Island in the Rideau alongside the Embassy. But a hundred and some years ago the island, named after John Porter, a Bytown civic engineer, was a place where those who were likely never to grow old were quarantined. For many years it doubled as a city dump, but in 1913 a smallpox hospital opened there, designed by Frank Sullivan, Ottawa's troubled Art Deco architect. The hospital closed in 1945, and in the mid-Sixties the increasing commercial exploitation of old age moved in. I try walking over to the island on a lovely steel frame pedestrian bridge but it is blocked both ends— surely somewhere else in the city there is a place for it, perhaps over to some other island. So I take the road more travelled. There is something edifying about living out your final years on an island, radical ions drifting from the water, and I almost consider signing up for when the day comes. I don't mind dying. I just don't want to be there when it happens.

The St. Patrick Street Bridge over to Beechwood is the equal in un-attractiveness to the Macdonald Cartier, completely functional. By contrast, in the distance upriver lies the beautiful Cummings Bridge in a picture postcard setting. We have a fine collection of bridges, and they appear at their best when given a 19th-century do-over, as in the Bank Street Bridge. And when you can see through them.

Stittsville Main Street

CPR Station in Stittvile, 1920.

*I*t doesn't befall many of us to have a town named after us, or even a hockey arena or a street. Some of you reading this may pull off one of the latter two, but the days when the former was possible have passed. The trick to it in these parts in the 19th century was to get somewhere ahead of the herd, get a mill or a general store going at a crossroads near water power, open the door and wait.

That is precisely what Jackson Stitt did, after arriving as part of the Irish tide in 1830, twenty-four years old and eager to make his mark. After hopscotching around the region, and marrying within a couple of years of his arrival, he switched from farming to merchanting and opened a tavern/general store combo at a crossroads that grew the name Stitt's Corners. He was named its first postmaster in 1854.

Jackson moved his five children and wife Ann into a home near his place of business, and they proceeded to add another eight children to their tally. When a large fire leveled the small hamlet he had cornered, plus a good deal of Carleton County, Stittsville wisely moved down to where the railway line was coming in. (Older bargain hunters will know where Stitt's Corners was when I say that the same site later hosted the Stittsville Flea Market, the main reason most of us ever went there. Apart from to retire.)

The Stittsville Main Street (I find the Stittsville a bit redundant; just plain Main Street would have saved on signage length and paint) is long, very long. It's more of a thoroughfare than a main street that has been stretched out.

Although the Main Street starts at the right-angled turn towards Ashton, I make the nearby Goulbourn Museum at Stanley's Corners my starting block and do a quick tour. A young summer student (from St. Catharines as it happened) leaves me to it, and in no time I've boned up on the progressive colonization of the local landscape. I learn that the town had trouble attracting doctors early on, and that the first telephone came into town in 1892 in a little booth in Mann's department store, where burly farmers lined up to bellow into the handset and tell everyone in earshot their news.

A hundred and twenty years later the descendants of those farmers are scattered all over town, thumb-twiddling as they walk, heads down, or talking to the air. Just about the only school's-out teenagers I don't see on a phone are erecting tents in front of the lovely, Norman Rockwell-esque Alexander Grove Community Centre, with Poole Creek burbling beside it.

Leaving the museum I work my way down the street numbers, slipping once through some handsome stone gates and finding myself in a fresh, barren field populated by half a dozen humungous homes, each different in style. How do these people make their money? Certainly not the way you or I do. These enclaves always carry names dedicated to the natural features that were eradicated to provide the ground to build on—for instance there is one called Deer Run here in Stittsville. Other lower-income-bracket mini-burbs sit beside main street, as do several mini-malls.

It's when I reach the Abbott crossroad that I realize I am in the heart of the village. The shade and benches of the small park on the southeast corner beckon, and I gradually notice that the park has a railway theme going, mostly aimed at youngsters, and indeed the Village Green Park was the former site of the railway station. Crossing the street, towards an older looking building, I discover an information stand, and learn that the first train came through on September 16th, 1870, one month after a great fire had floored the town, apart from a handful of buildings (the still standing Hartin House predates the fire) and forced the town to shift position. The station lasted almost a century before it was demolished. It was a sad, snowy day, January 14th, 1990, when the last VIA came through on its way west. The next day crews arrived to begin tearing up the track. Almost immediately the town, including the venerable Bradley family, got behind having the Trans-Canada trail occupy the old track bed, and a decade later it did. I can see it stretching off in either direction, a narrow dirt path running through with trees hugging the sides. It looks delightful and inviting and worth a walk along someday.

Elsewhere in the heart of the village I winkle out a couple of historical plaques, less fancy than those in Ottawa and put up by the local historical society. They include: one to a blacksmith; one where the first bank opened in a duplex next to a grocery store, and one on the old Butler House built right by the railway. Butler opened a hotel there in 1894 to catch the railway trade, but when his daughter was ironically killed by a train he moved away.

The place swapped pushing booze for pumping out ice cream when prohibition came to the county in 1907, and it remains in commercial hands.

Main Street Stittsville did get a sprucing up in the couple of years after the railway tracks disappeared. Old style lampposts were brought in, and the sidewalk concrete has been etched in strips to resemble a boardwalk. As in so many other smaller Ontario towns, the main street is a checkerboard of older buildings, some left to age gracefully, others given a facade-lift that rarely improves them, alongside modern homes and businesses.

Vernon

Osgoode Baptist & Vernon United Church.

riving southeast down Highway 31 is unpleasant. Bottled up on Bank, eyes right past Lansdowne, endless retail overkill both sides, treadmill through the car lots, quick flit of green in a graveyard, new and soon-to-be-new dormitory suburbs with ironic names lifted from nature, trailer lots, a dead restaurant or two, into Greeley, low swampy bush waiting to turn into suburbs, a sign for Marvelville Road, where the superheroes live, finally, thirty kilometres from the Peace Tower, past the Metcalfe sign and the lights at Snake Island Road, the first sightings of working barns and silos and fields, and the existential, grinding hum starts to turn into a pastoral melody.

Ten kilometres more, stop at the roadside farm store for local honey—save the bees! — and the sign says *Welcome To Vernon*. A minute later I'm out the other side and across the Ottawa border. Pull a U, and I park for absolutely free, for as long as I want, outside the library, which looks like an old one-room schoolhouse, because it was. A large tile set in the wall above the porch dates it at 1882, which is like, totally pre-smart phone. Standing at the roadside, with a nearby fenced-in barking dog posing as a burglar alarm, there are three churches at one end of the village, a convenience store in the middle, and a museum at the other.

The village of Vernon was in Osgoode Township prior to the Great Amalgamation of 2001, and it was then, and still is, a quiet place, with its rural quota of communal tragedies and dramas, crimes and blessings. The church with the highest spire, visible from a tractor seat anywhere in the surrounding fields, and the tallest building in town, which dates from 1887, is Presbyterian. The lady vicar's name is Chan, and there is a discarded beer can in the parking lot. How Canadian is that? The Anglican and Baptist churches are opposite each other, a minute's walk from the Presbyterian; the Baptists are advertising their Harvest Festival, which makes sense out here, where there actually is a harvest.

Judging by the dates on the primary buildings in Vernon, it was on the up and up in the 1880s, and leveled out somewhere along the line, with the older farm houses and retired farming homes on the west side , and some newer semi-suburban homes on the east. The functional community centre, with a billboard outside it welcoming army cadets, is relatively new. While I'm outside a young woman in a teddy bear outfit runs out to her car and back. Halloween teddy bears picnic?

For me the heart of the village is the Osgoode Township Museum, which got going in the early-'70s and is run by good, active folks and includes an Agricultural Museum. A plaque outside informs me that Alexander Rutherford, who was born in Osgoode in 1857, went west as a young man and ended up as the first Premier of Alberta. Well, well. I've given several talks at the museum, and enjoyed my visits with people who take their neighbours in time seriously, and who have good, how-it-used-to-be stories of their own to pass on.

The only curiosity in town is a Chinese temple in a one-story building, an ex-general store I suspect, with five enlarged historical photographs of Vernon pinned to the façade. There is not a word of English anywhere on it. According to Farid, the pleasant man who has run the convenience store for the last twelve years, the temple landed here a few months ago, and keeps itself to itself, as does the village. Meanwhile, the Ottawa suburbs, and the world in general, get closer to Vernon every year. Hopefully, they will be slow in coming.

Wellington Street West

Parkdale Park adjacent to Parkdale Market.

*I*f you pull up the map of downtown Ottawa, and run your finger westward along Wellington, starting at the Chateau Laurier, a funny thing happens. Past the Park of the Provinces, beloved of skateboarders, the street doglegs left, runs down a little, then dead ends at Pooley's Bridge on LeBreton Flats, by the 1875 pumping station. (Pooley's is Ottawa's very first bridge, originally simply fashioned from felled logs and built by Lieutenant Henry Pooley, Colonel By's second-in-command, around 1826; upgraded to stone in 1836.)

You can pick Wellington up again by hopping your finger over to the other side of LeBreton Flats. It starts up again at the back of the City Centre. It is here, on the corner of Breezehill and Wellington, that I decide to start my ramble along the Duke of Wellington's highway, which passes through a couple of Ottawa's more hoody neighbourhoods. The Wellington Street section that runs past Parliament and all those federal buildings feels more national than local to me, so I will skip that part.

The western stretch of Wellington has a distinctly inauspicious start, at a chain link fence corralling the City Centre and then it runs along a short ways to meet Bayswater. As I am walking this, I suddenly recall what had stood on the vacant ground to my right; the lumberyard of Kemp Edwards, which had the best offcuts for purchase in the city. It was a family business, run by descendants of William Edwards, who got here very early, had a thriving mill, and at one time owned 24 Sussex.

The other side of Bayswater, in the 900 block of Wellington, begins with two businesses devoted to the motorcar, and then a priest steps out of a small house, the St. Jude's drop-in centre. This sets up the feel for this part of the neighbourhood—a mixture of cars, Catholicism and commercialism. The real estate around here is modest, and, I have to say, one can tell from the increase in the percentage of visible minorities, as the census form calls them, that are, um, visible. This also makes strolling the sidewalks past the local retail and restaurants, where you might be invited to "get your smoke on" or sample natural toys in the space of a few steps, eclectically and ethnically interesting.

Trapped between Somerset and Wellington there is a small triangular park and it is here, modestly placed in among the renovations, I find the bronze plaque telling me I am in Hintonburg, and that Joseph Hinton founded the village in 1893.

It was annexed by the ever-spreading Ottawa in 1907. Hinton, a shopkeeper, had actually been dead almost a decade when the village took his name in perpetuity, but his civic contributions, including landing a post office and a town hall, are worthily remembered.

A few feet beyond Hinton's plaque I stand and study a white marble fire hydrant with a corncob emerging from it. Like Preston Street, Wellington has recently acquired a selection of staggered sidewalk sculptures, courtesy of artists Marcus Kucey Jones and Ryan Lotecki. To my eye, they lighten the streetscape, and watching them age will become a neighbourhood pasttime.

On the other hand I'm not so keen on this habit of flying branding banners from lampposts, which has also broken out along Wellington since they did an otherwise fine job of sprucing up the sidewalks—widening them, inserting olde-style lampposts, benches, trees. Communities don't need branding; they are not businesses, they are homes. They'll be hiring professional greeters next.

The sheer glorious bulk of Église Saint-François-d'Assise puts a smile on my face as I stand before it; the sun warms both it and me, heathen humanist that I am. The Capuchin Fathers oversaw the building of the first parish church in 1890, and this version went up even as World War I had just kicked off. I particularly like the non-matching bell towers, and the statue of St. Francis on the façade. Francis, named for his father's love of France, led quite the life, choosing to live poorly, founding an order for senior women, befriending a Muslim sultan, and urging compassion not contempt for the natural world. A man for our times as well as his own.

Rising from the steps of the church, and pointing my face into the spring sun reaching the street without hindrance from high rises, I walk on down Wellington. The street is named after the British warrior and Prime Minister known as the Iron Duke, an Anglo-Irishman by birth. Wellington the militarist, then Master General of the Board of Ordnance, conceived of the need for a colonial canal between the Rideau River and the St. Lawrence, and dispatched one Colonel By in 1826 to make it so. Two years later, Wellington was both Prime Minister and First Lord of the Treasury (not a bad job) and secured the money to make the canal possible. Colonel By returned the favour, when laying out the nascent Bytown, by naming one of its two primary streets after his employer. And I have a pair of his boots.

Within a few steps I arrive at the Elmdale Tavern, music hall and social focal point on this stretch of Wellington, one of the few hostelries in town that feels like a true tavern—the old separate entrances for big boys and girls, like a school, still evident. Half a wall in the pool table room is covered with black and white pictures of the neighbourhood as it was in the Fifties; these include snapshots of vanished businesses such as the Dominion grocery store, Jo's Confectionary (a word you don't see much anymore, whereas "cupcakery" is on the ascendancy) and the Wong Sing Chinese Laundry. The Elmdale itself started out as the 1909 home and dry goods store of Earnest Laroche, converting to a tavern as the Depression was waning in 1934. It is also a historical fact that Prime Minister Chrétien, after a basketball game, refreshed himself in the Elmdale one afternoon and chatted with the assembled wise and worldly. It may or may not be a coincidence, but shortly after that visit, the PM decided not to send Canadian troops into Iraq.

Exiting the tavern, unfortunately as non-alcoholic as I entered it, a pleasant smell of pizza cooked in a wood-fired oven assails me as I cross the street to check out another building sporting a heritage plaque. Sadly, the plaque is the only thing in good repair on the building, a once fine stone-faced home. It was built in 1881 for a man with the good Ottawa name of Francis Magee and saw service as a series of banks. It received heritage status in 1996, and I hope to hear of its rejuvenation soon, for it presents a sad face to the street just now.

Right next door, at 1121, is one of Ottawa's prettiest shop fronts, complete with stained glass over the windows and a curved glass entrance reminiscent of the Holt Renfrew building in Montreal. It rises however to a curious false façade that appears to add another floor but there is nothing behind it. The Queen Anne style building, in fact an early example of the architecture of W. E. Noffke, on the corner at Rosemount, completes a very pleasant mixed-bag run of architecture.

The quiet Catholic-style building at 1153 Wellington a block down, past the Community Support Building with its pre-emptive plastic sunflowers in the flower bed, has long intrigued me, for the stories it holds within. On the lawn in front, between two as yet unleafed trees, there is a large plaque with the words HOME CHILDREN in capitals and beneath them is the remarkable news that this slightly shabby building was once known as the St. George's Home.

Between 1869 and 1948 multiple generations of children from the British Isles, dispatched to Canada by charities dealing with abandoned, orphaned or unwanted boys and girls, were barracked in "homes" like this one before being shipped off, mostly westward, to farms and rural homesteads to work as child labour. In all, the estimate is that around 100,000 children came to Canada in those eight decades, and I can happily report that a selection of their stories has been compiled and put into a book called *British Home Children*. One of the entries in the book tells the tale of Kenneth Donovan, who spent some time in the St. George's Home (which closed in 1934), before heading off to a farm from which he ran away, being placed again on another farm in Manotick. Kenneth the grown man settled in Ottawa, had a civil service career and died in 2004. He was fond of saying, "If you can't do Canada any good, please don't do it any harm."

As I proceed along the wide sidewalk I glance over to the Grace Manor, a rest home now and part of the Salvation Army Complex but once the site of the hospital where many an Ottawan got their start. The hospital shifted over from Sandy Hill in 1922, and grew a pair of wings until, despite a vigorous Save the Grace campaign, the much-loved old Sally Ann Building closed in 1999. There is a vibrant Irish bar, named after one of the city's more genteel founding Irish families in the 1200 block with a great open stage night and weekend live music, which is as things should be. You can walk through the '60's-style diner next door into a surprise bowling alley.

After looking in the window of the Ju-jitsu dojo at small people half my size and twenty times my agility jousting with hanging bags, I flick a bird at the gas prices on display at the station of the corner of Parkdale, and continue west. The corner of Holland and Wellington is one of my favourites in the city, excepting the bank on the corner; the German playwright Bertolt Brecht once said that it may well be as great a crime to own a bank as it is to rob one. On the other three corners there is a vegetarian restaurant, a map store for the idle planning of global getaways, and the Great Canadian Theatre Company's home; who could ask for anything more? I'm sure the ghost of Jane Jacobs, a smile on its face, walks this part of Wellington from time to time.

Jane Jacobs had a Yoda sort of appearance, and a fearless intelligence that she focused on the errant planning of New York in particular and later large North American cities in general. She poured her powerful thoughts into a book—*The Death and Life of Great American Cities.* Eventually she quit the States and became Canadian, and prevented Toronto from doing the ugly on several occasions. I was blessed to interview her once before her death in 2006, and was greatly and permanently affected by her wise words, written and spoken. She is a guiding spirit, and I never leave home without her when chronicling Ottawa on these pages.

One of the great planning errors in her estimation was homogeneity, the crushing of diversity along streets by modern development. The quartet of elements that she figured gave rise to positive "streetness" were: mixed uses, short blocks, buildings of various ages and states of repair and density. I would add compassion for the pedestrian, and the almost complete absence of buildings more than five stories high. The Wellington I've been walking down these last three weeks has all of these, which is why I would probably vote highly for it in a Most Walkable Street in Ottawa contest.

Allowing Ms. Jacobs' ghost to take my arm, we leave the Parkdale intersection and, after checking to see that the neighbourhood bookstore has her writings in stock, we high-step into the St. Vincent de Paul and emerge with a couple of shining summer shirts, now that local warming is upon us.

For the next two blocks the street is thick with the smell of food, of baking and butchers, herbs and spices, pasta and pickles and such. A quick bagel in the no-nonsense restaurant and deli proves irresistible, and there is a smile-inducing art exhibition within, which an explanatory sheet on a pillar tells me is the work of the artistic members of H'Art of Ottawa, an organization and studio that encourages self-expression in Ottawans with developmental disabilities. To a canvas, the works are joyfully bright and seem to bloom on the walls rather than hang. The paintings provide a contrast-and-compare opportunity with the group show on display in the windows of the nearby Cube gallery, which has as its subject Ottawa's alleyways, and which is also well worth a stare.

Moving on, there is an array of locally grown or made and organic nourishment available that highlights the ever-growing healthy food revolution. Actually, the revolution seems more reactionary in nature, if one credits the saying that if you want to eat well these days, eat like your great-grandmother, who ate from a plate not under siege by Big Food.

The garage on the southeast corner of the intersection with Island Park is historical in its own right, and offers a fitting end to Wellington. Its Thirties, slightly Art Deco appearance is genuine; it opened in December 1938 as the entrepreneurial endeavour of Messieurs. Gaw and Egan, back when gas was 10 cents a gallon and a new car was less than $1000 and minimum wage, which the pump jockeys no doubt made, was forty cents.

At Island Park, actually one street past, the Duke of Wellington hands over to the Duke of Richmond (who was Governor-General from 1818-20), and Richmond Road makes its way westward all the way to the hamlet of, no surprise, Richmond, which pre-dates Ottawa.

Wilbrod Street

The century old École Francojeunesse Pavillon at 339 Wilbrod.
Will it survive?

*S*ome parts of Ottawa are more walkable than others; the riverside pathways provide an opportunity for waterside reflective thinking and an increased ionic intake. If the purpose of your stroll is some light retail therapy, then you may well head for the sidewalks of the Glebe or Westboro (although the western end of the Wellington/Richmond retail strip is turning into an unattractive wind tunnel). Personally, as an amateur student of the city's architecture, both ugly (lots of that) and beautiful (endangered), when I find myself in need of a dose of consistent attractive, I point my feet along an east-west running street in Sandy Hill.

Clearly others think Sandy Hill's architectural integrity worth preserving, because in 1982 the City acknowledged the residential wish that the Wilbrod Street Heritage Conservation District be created, and the integrity regulations that go with a designation like that have since come into play.

Essentially that means it is harder for the Big Ugly to ride in and pillage Sandy Hill, which is a good thing, and indeed why would you want to crap on those lovely avenues and Second Empire façades and history, except if you were profiteering?

Wilbrod Street takes its name from the eldest son of Louis-Théodore Besserer, who was a notary by training, later a militia soldier and, in his still later years in Ottawa, a real estate profiteer. By the time Besserer arrived in Bytown from Quebec City in 1845, he was a discontent sixty-year-old man, his wife having recently died. His political opponents in Montreal were glad to see him retired and gone. Louis-Théodore came to Ottawa because almost two decades earlier he had inherited a land grant Colonel By had given to his brother René, who died relatively young. The grant was a sizable estate in the undeveloped southeast corner of Bytown, which consisted mostly of a flat-topped hill topped with a sandy soil. Those acres turned out to make the Besserer family a heap of money.

Once he had his own house up and running on what is now King Edward, on the crown of the hill, Besserer subdivided his estate and laid out a grid of streets, one of which bears his nom de famille. He made considerable money from selling lots, mainly to well-heeled Catholics, before he died in 1861, by which time Ottawa had become the capital, and his twelve children subsequently made a whole lot more. I lived in Sandy Hill in the late 1980s, in an attic apartment, and often strolled the streets, dodging hasty students late for class and handing out cheap gloves in winter to gentlemen from the halfway house. The street

I visited least in those days was Wilbrod, which is why I set out down it last week.

Wilbrod starts on the eastern side of Cumberland; the dainty portion to the west of that, running up to Waller, is Séraphin-Marion, which lies in Ottawa University territory. That block is itself full of history, literally, as part of the university's history department is there. The impressive Academic Hall once contained a natural history museum, and now houses the oldest extant theatre in the region, which went up in 1923.

There are lots of people going in and out of St. Joseph's Church on the southeast corner of Wilbrod and Cumberland, clutching cards, and it takes a moment and some signage reading to figure out that it is not a June wedding—they are voters. It is Ontario Election Day and St. Joe's is a polling station, hence the temporary, finished-the-day-before wheelchair ramp. I poke my head in and realize I'm making the stewards nervous with my apolitical, historical curiosity, so I exit.

The story goes that the first church dedicated to St. Joseph in Sandy Hill (corner of Wilbrod and Cumberland) was built alongside a graveyard for the slain workers on the Rideau Canal, and that the bells of the first small stone church on the site were the first to ring out in Ottawa. I'll take both as gospel. The present building is built on the salvaged foundation of the one that burnt almost to the ground in 1930. It's an active, welcoming church, still one of the roots of the community.

A little further east on the opposing side sits the more compact St. Paul's, with something familiar about its façade. There is a hint of Art Deco to the flanking additions either side of the red doors, and I recall that W. E. Noffke, one of Ottawa's more outstanding architectural stylists (think white walls and tiled semi-Spanish roofs) had done the additions of his beloved church. Turn around, and there is the first house that Noffke, freshly married at the age of 25, designed and lived in, starting in 1903. Truth to tell the house, a brown, not well-attended-to dwelling, is no great shakes, utterly unlike his later work. But he dreamed of grander things within it, and achieved them.

Crossing King Edward and noting, because of the tinkling bell that sounds directly behind me, that Wilbrod has a dedicated free-wheeling bike path, Route 2 east, I gaze longingly at an empty swimming pool affiliated with a drab low-rise apartment block. A sign at one end reads *No Long Deep Dives*. Solid advice, in life and in bathing.

It is always a joy to discover something new on these strolls of mine, and that happens next. Though I have walked here several times, I had not noticed Cornwall, a right-angled, quiet-mixed-bag cul-de-sac that heads south on the south side. I envy those living on it, and pause a while to eavesdrop on a pair of friends, one of whom plays blues guitar while the other explains the virtues of his brand new Jaguar.

Thereafter there is a sheer pleasantness to strolling along Wilbrod. (It is a perfect early summer day, so I am easily delighted). Sight and smell are entertaining rather than offensive, and the exterior activities of the inhabitants make for fine theatre, although the underlying tension between town and gown, student and resident, is there. This is evident in two houses, one on the north side, the other directly across on the south. On the south side, three beer-toting students on a porch are watching the World Cup on a computer, roaring their team on, while a quiet, ivy-covered mansion with iron railings and a conservatory sits in mute rebuke.

For long stretches of Wilbrod, the architecture and flora in Sandy Hill harmonize, and all is peaceful. But the new city order is gradually invading it, certainly there are more and more of those nouvelle mode, minimalist slim wood, steel and concrete infill homes that are all right angles and pop up all over town. It makes me wish that a by-law could be passed tomorrow making it just plain wrong to knock down a perfectly good building, or cut down a healthy tree.

After passing a small corner collection of stores—barber shop, laundry with those two guys in chairs in front that seem placed there by ordnance, coffee shop, pets, organics and a school of a brick Art Deco design (I collect and treasure Ottawa's shallow stock of Art Deco buildings). I pause outside a small steep-roofed home painted a deep glorious matte red. A black maple leaf in bas-relief stands out over the door. I attach no sign of the times to the leaf's black and the present state of federal governance but instead take it as a sort of permanent Canada Day symbol. Which day is tomorrow, and I wish you and the country a restful or a rowdy one, depending on your inclination.

All the gardens in front of the big, very big, houses on Wilbrod east of Chapel are looking terrific in the sunshine after a couple of days of heavy rain. Several of the mansions are embassies and their attendant residencies, including the beige Brazilian embassy where a man is quietly harvesting grass cuttings at the side, while the staff within are perhaps still weeping into their keyboards over the last soccer world cup result.

After a small detour down Augusta to give a nod to the house where Lester Pearson once lived while attempting to make Canada one of the world's grown-up countries, I return to Wilbrod and I can hear chattering but the only other person on the street is the mail deliverer, who I realize is on one of those phone-in-the-ear things. This is obviously a well-worn route for her. She slips through the gate of a sedate home with an iron railing fence backed up by a hedge to be greeted by a madly barking dog. "Hello, Daisy" she says and the dog goes quiet. How much longer they will be greeting each other is a moot, Canada Post executive decision.

Next door to a house undergoing renovation, where a workman has the radio up to bird-stunning volume, is a relatively plain grey house set well back, with a brass plaque beside the door. The plaque tells me that none other than General Charles de Gaulle visited here on July 14th, 1944; exactly seventy years ago. The house was then the Canadian HQ of the provisional government of the Republic of France, awaiting liberation. On one of President de Gaulle's later visits in 1960, he was not as warmly greeted in Ottawa as he was in Quebec.

More big houses, more embassies, Guinea, Romania, more gardens to stand and ponder—is there a more trustworthy un-killable plant than the hosta? — and then I am at Charlotte. To my right the Russian Embassy is quiet on the outside and no doubt busy processing mega data on the inside.

The other side of Charlotte consists of a tidy row of town houses on the north side and one heck of a home on the south at number 500. It's a terracotta masterpiece of turrets and tiling and fancy brickwork. Though it is now the Algerian Embassy, this palatial place has been the repository of quite a chunk of Ottawa history. The long-lived lumber baron, J. R. Booth had the house built for his daughter and her husband, and got the Ottawa architect and artist John Watts to design it. It took two years to build and was completed in 1903. The lumber barons liked to have their houses built with a river view (as Bronson did at the end of Wellington), and the husband, Andrew Fleck, who managed some of Booth's mills and his railway, the Canadian Atlantic, no doubt enjoyed a few cigars with the view. Fleck became a major local philanthropist in his later years— you'll recognize the Andrew Fleck Child Care services.

Gertrude Fleck stayed in the house till 1940, then sold to a Senator, Norman Paterson, who was in there until his death in 1983, aged ninety-nine. A couple of developers took a go at doing something with it, but then the Maharishi Heaven on Earth Development Corporation picked it up and spirited a lot of money into it before giving up and it went into its present incarnation. The selling price to the Algerians was a local real estate record, but then what's money?

The only building after the Fleck-Patterson house is a retirement home that stands in what were once the Fleck/ Patterson grounds. I envy the residents their view, and consider sneaking into a gazebo for an eyeful across the Rideau River into Vanier, when I hear the mail deliverer again and see that she has paused by a gated set of steps leading down to a small patio overlooking the river. A sign the other side of the gate says this is public access, but a passing member of the home's staff doesn't think it is any more. Down I go anyway, to this journey's end at the River of History.

Is Ottawa a Walkable City?

Ottawa in 1940 as seen from Hull, Quebec.

"If the public realm, where the buildings
meet the sidewalk, is activated, this
demonstrates that a New World city can
remain alive despite the formal idiocies of
Modernist urban theory and practice."

— *Jane Jacobs, 2000*

Not long ago, on a cool, cloudy, drizzly day, I had the honour of being a walking, talking part of an event called Jane's Walks, which saw hundreds of people over a weekend walking parts of the city with a guide. The Jane in that title refers to Jane Jacobs, and she was a sort of existential patron saint of North American cities. A quick sketch of her theory to do with city streets will get us to the point of understanding why her life has inspired a bunch of walks, not just in Ottawa but in five other Canadian cites and a growing flock of American ones.

In 1961, Jacobs published a book called *The Death and Life of Great American Cities* and eventually it gave the same smack upside the head to the theory of city planning that Rachel Carson's *Silent Spring* did on pesticide use. I say theory because, while Carson's book actually made a moratorium on DDT use happen, Jacob's book slowed down and diverted a lot of city planners from making sterile downtown streets but she didn't put a halt to it, and hence we still are cursed, for instance, with the Sparks Street Mall at night.

After many years of observation in the U.S. Jacobs, who was self-instructed and literally very street-smart, came up with what she called an ecology of cities. Meaning what? Well, among many other things that make up the unique eco-system that is a modern city, she divided the citizens into two rough groups—the car people and the foot people. The car people had seized the minds of planners, she said, and the foot people had been left behind. But the foot people had managed to keep a toehold on certain streets, like Greenwich Village in New York, the neighbourhood wherein she wrote her groundbreaking book.

In a foreword Jacobs wrote in 1992 to *The Death and Life of Great American Cities*, when she was living in Toronto, her adopted home and the city where she died in 2006, she had this to say: "Some people prefer doing their workaday errands on foot, or feel they would like to if they lived in a place where they could. Other people prefer hopping into the car to do errands, or would like to if they had a car. In a kind of shorthand, we can speak of foot people and car people." She then said that her book was, "instantly understood by foot people, both actual and wishful. They recognized that what it said jived with their own enjoyment, concerns...the book collaborated with foot people by giving legitimacy to what they already knew for themselves. Experts of the time did not respect what foot people knew and valued. They were deemed old-fashioned and selfish—troublesome sand in the wheels of progress."

What she was talking about has come to be known as "walkability," which is a way of judging how conducive a street is to the social of act of walking it. It would take a newspaper page, not a column, to expand on that, but it has to do with a good healthy density, a useful, pleasing mixture of non-big box, non-global franchise retail, a secure feeling while out promenading, some eye-catching eccentricity, or what might be called character, and so on. Again, she puts it better: "Wherever one sees stretches of old city buildings," she writes, "that have been usefully recycled for new and different purposes; wherever sidewalks have been widened and vehicular roadways narrowed precisely where they should be—on streets in which pedestrian traffic is bustling and plentiful; wherever downtowns are not deserted after their offices close; wherever new, fine-grained mixtures of street uses have been fostered successfully; wherever new buildings have been sensitively inserted among old ones to knit up holes and tatters in a city neighbourhood so that the mending is all but invisible."

So, all that said, which parts of Ottawa can be said to adhere or come close to the description Jacobs provides in the paragraph I just quoted? Or, to put it on another footing, which are the most walkable parts of town? Agreed, that is a subjective thing; it could be just a numerical foot count of the throng or lack of it of street people, by which I mean people socializing on the street of a midweek evening, but it is more than that. It is a state of communal mind, not numbers, a sort of voting with your feet that fills the street and makes it a destination.

My Top Six

*I*n the hope that it will spark debate, both among the car people and the foot people, here's my Top Six parts of the city with high walkability. Of course, the best way of determining if they are also your Top Six is for you to walk them. And to rack up as many Jane's Walks as you can. Bonne promenade.

WELLINGTON WEST FROM BAYSWATER TO CHURCHILL

Saint Francis of Assisi

Despite the arrival of the condosaurus at the western end of this walk, and the wind tunnel effect it leaves behind, this is probably the best stretch of window gazing in the city. My favourites are the St. Vincent de Paul, where objects from Ottawa past fill the storefront. A light went out with the passing of the Cube Gallery, which often had Ottawa art in the windows. Glance up as I pass Saint Francis of Assisi with its mismatched steeple and tower, and whose five bells have rung the births deaths and marriages of Wellington Village for close to a century.

Also, music to my ears, there are several live music venues along the way, although the de-grunged, quieter Elmdale Tavern was once where the music never died. Whatever your opinion of public art, there at least is some along the street in fine white marble, and sufficient bench-ery for pit stops and enjoying the world as it goes by, which it always does. The storefronts, which display a great retail diversity, have mostly managed to avoid homogeneity, and there are any number of ways to treat your appetite.

GLEBE-OTTAWA SOUTH FROM QUEENSWAY TO BREWER PARK

Patterson Creek

I usually start this one with a walkabout in Patterson Creek, then south on Bank with glances left and right at the David Younghusband homes, and maybe with a refresher stop in Wild Oats. Crossing the lovely retro Bank Street Bridge, maybe a once-around Brown's Inlet, and then down past the reassuring endurance of the Mayfair cinema and along the Canadian Folk Music Walk of Fame, whose title is almost as long as the walk itself.

More than one antique/second-hand store along here, which I can never resist. Quick memory movie as I pass where the Strand Cinema used to be, and then I'm at the Rideau at the north end of the Billings Bridge, the first incarnation of which was built in 1831. There is a park to the left of me, and a park to the right.

RIDEAU FROM BYTOWNE CINEMA TO STRATHCONA PARK

The Bytowne

Starting at one of my most visited blocks, which hosts a repertory cinema, previously enjoyed bookstore and music supplies emporium, I'll head east and indulge in some serious people watching. Perhaps a quiet hour in the library, filling in my gaps in Canadian history. There is diversity galore along here, both in ethnic dining and language eavesdropping.

Past the old armoury, now apartments, and carry on over the Rideau River via Cummings Bridge, where the island on the right once held Mr. Cummings store, and then right at the end into Riverain Park. From Riverain

I take the relatively new pedestrian bridge, the Adàwe Crossing, to save having to wade across, as in days of old, and into Strathcona Park, now a park catering to all ages, but once a rifle range, then Ottawa's first golf course.

PRESTON FROM PLANT BATH TO COMMISSIONERS PARK

Preston St at Gladstone Ave.

A great stroll, including houses of laughter and multiple styles of lasagna. Eating your way from one end to other would be a gastronomic odyssey, mainly catering to la dolce vita, but with some Asian and a touch of New Orleans. Usually a soccer game in progress at the intersection with Gladstone. Always there is something I need in Preston hardware. Pause to observe bunches of men in cafes, fixing our broken world one espresso at a time.

The underpass for the Queensway is a history lesson, as are the mostly granite, adult-sized public art obelisks dotted along the sidewalk, anchored to the pavement along the street. The kitsch of the Pub Italia window is always worth a look. Passing under the Little Italy Arch, you are tiptoeing through the tulips in Commissioners Park.

CHINATOWN ALONG SOMERSET

Detail of Chinatown arch

When I was a boy, Little China-town was on Albert Street but starting in the early-70s it began to snake out along Somerset. I start this stroll in Dundonald Park, leaning on Igor Gouzenko's plaque. Then westward along Somerset, with a nasal nod to the Shanghai, the progenitor of Chinatown. Once safely across

Bronson, both nostrils widen as I pass under the arch, the Royal Arch to give it its full name, with its 1,000-year-old coin embedded in it somewhere. Enter the dragon, so to speak.

I have occasionally seen a Dominican monk from the nearby Dominican University College on the streets while I immerse myself in quite, grabbing some pho noodles. Try and decipher the characters from the world's oldest language. The only one I know is the one for compassion.

NATIONAL ARTS CENTRE TO NEPEAN POINT

Algonquin hunter

The path heading along the Canal north away from the Arts Centre takes me under the Plaza Bridge, a space that was brilliantly opened up a few years ago, revealing some of the original foundation stones of Ottawa's first bridge, Sappers'. Then alongside the locks down to the small but powerful Bytown Museum (for which I wrote and recorded the audio guide.) Retrace my steps and ascend the stone staircase onto Wellington, then a short walk to the steps down to the Chateau Laurier terrace, out the other end into Major's Hill park, where once a cannon was fired at noon daily, and the ladies and gentleman of the street take their naps.

Pay my respects to the statue of the Algonquin hunter that used to sit at the foot of Champlain's statue on Nepean Point and now has a corner of his own in the park. Exit the park at the north end, cross the street and amble up to Nepean Point, where Champlain is staring upriver with his upside down astrolabe. Best vista in town. If it's Thursday after five, maybe a free visit to the National Gallery and a quiet half-hour with beautiful singing in the Rideau Chapel.

Acknowledgements

The *Ottawa Citizen* gave me permission to gather these street stories into this book. My thanks to all my *Citizen* editors over the course of twenty-five years of articling — in particular David Watson and Christina Spencer.

The wonderful cover is by my illustrative friend, Albert Prisner, a fellow walker.

My buddy Ken Ginn initially prepared the illustrations. Magdalene Carson's final design is all an author could wish for.

Frances Curry went above and beyond prepping and polishing my rough drafts. Couldn't have done it without you.

Dear friend Kae McColl gave the book a superb copy edit. Cheers, Kae.

And I am of course sincerely grateful to publisher Ron Corbett for deciding to get behind my book, and push.

About the Author

ince 1978, after emigrating from Liverpool, England, and returning to Ottawa where he grew up in the 1950s, Phil Jenkins has worked as a newspaper columnist, travel writer, author and a performing songwriter across Canada. He was a freelance columnist for the *Ottawa Citizen* from 1991 to 2017. He has written for over forty magazines, including *National Geographic, Traveller, Equinox, Wedding Bells, Canadian Geographic, Ottawa Magazine* and *Toronto Life,* and about the Canadian landscape in the non-fiction bestsellers *Fields of Vision: A Journey to Canada's Family Farms, An Acre of Time, River Song: Sailing the History of the St. Lawrence* and *Beneath My Feet: The Memoirs of George Mercer Dawson.* Also two commissioned histories, of the Ottawa Public Library and the Ottawa Civic Heart Institute. Phil teaches and lectures in writing and Ottawa history and culture. As a solo musician, songwriter and member of the band Riverbend, he has produced the albums *Car Tunes, Making Waves* and *Noteworthy.* He lives in the Gatineau Hills of Quebec.

Printed in Great Britain
by Amazon

57796712R00144